RUGBY
Games & Drills

RUGBY
Games & Drills

**RUGBY
FOOTBALL
UNION**

Simon Worsnop

Human Kinetics

Library of Congress Cataloging-in-Publication Data

Rugby games & drills / RFU ; Simon Worsnop [contributor].
   p. cm.
  Includes bibliographical references.
  ISBN-13: 978-1-4504-0213-2 (soft cover)
  ISBN-10: 1-4504-0213-5 (soft cover)
 1. Rugby football--Coaching. 2. Rugby football--Training. I. Worsnop, Simon. II.
Rugby Football Union. III. Title: Rugby games and drills.
  GV945.75.R84 2012
  796.333--dc23

                         2011021474

  ISBN-10: 1-4504-0213-5 (print)
  ISBN-13: 978-1-4504-0213-2 (print)

Acquisitions Editor: Peter Murphy; **Developmental Editor:** Laura Floch; **Assistant Editor:** Elizabeth Evans; **Copyeditor:** John Wentworth; **Permissions Manager:** Martha Gullo; **Graphic Designer:** Bob Reuther; **Cover Designer:** Keith Blomberg; **Photographer (cover):** David Rogers/Getty Images; **Photographer (interior):** pp. 1, 15, 35, 47, 91, 127 ©RFU/Russell Cheyne; pp. 67, 167 ©RFU/Paul Seiser; p. 103 ©RFU/Leo Wilkinson; p. 157 ©RFU; **Photo Asset Manager:** Laura Fitch; **Visual Production Assistant:** Joyce Brumfield; **Photo Production Manager:** Jason Allen; **Art Manager:** Kelly Hendren; **Associate Art Manager:** Alan L. Wilborn; **Illustrations:** © Human Kinetics; **Printer:** Sheridan Books

Human Kinetics books are also available at special discounts for bulk purchase. Special editions or book excerpts can also be created to specification. For details, contact the Special Sales Manager at Human Kinetics.

Printed in the United States of America   10 9 8 7 6 5 4 3 2 1

The paper in this book is certified under a sustainable forestry program.

Human Kinetics
Website: www.HumanKinetics.com

United States: Human Kinetics
P.O. Box 5076
Champaign, IL 61825-5076
800-747-4457
e-mail: humank@hkusa.com

Canada: Human Kinetics
475 Devonshire Road Unit 100
Windsor, ON N8Y 2L5
800-465-7301 (in Canada only)
e-mail: info@hkcanada.com

Europe: Human Kinetics
107 Bradford Road
Stanningley
Leeds LS28 6AT, United Kingdom
+44 (0) 113 255 5665
e-mail: hk@hkeurope.com

Australia: Human Kinetics
57A Price Avenue
Lower Mitcham, South Australia 5062
08 8372 0999
e-mail: info@hkaustralia.com

New Zealand: Human Kinetics
P.O. Box 80
Torrens Park, South Australia 5062
0800 222 062
e-mail: info@hknewzealand.com

E5303

To my mother and father for giving me a good start and to Carys and Josie for making me such a proud dad—*S.W.*

Contents

Game and Drill Finder

Game or Drill title	Page #	Number of players		Handling: Catching and passing	Handling: Decision making	Kicking	Defensive organization	Team attack	Team defense
		Small group	Team						
Chapter 2 Small-Sided Handling Games									
Running Tag	18	■		■					
Rob the Nest	19	■		■					
Rob the Den	20	■		■					
Circle Dodge Ball	21	■		■					
Air Catch	22	■		■					
Lift and Catch	23	■		■					
Keep Ball	24	■		■	■				
Keep Ball Variation	25	■		■	■				
Keep Ball Contact Variation	26	■		■	■				
Ball Tag	27	■		■	■				
Fifth Columnist	28	■		■	■				
Hit the Cone	29	■		■	■				
End Corner Ball	30	■		■	■				
Mixed Corner Ball	31	■		■	■				
Mat Ball	32	■		■	■				
Rugby Netball	33	■		■	■				
Channel Ball	34	■		■	■				
Chapter 3 Small-Sided Kicking Games									
Kick Out	37	■				■			
Target Defence	38	■				■			
Beat the Guards	39	■				■			
Hit the Cone	40	■		■		■			
Team Skittles	41	■		■		■			
Rugby Soccer	42	■		■	■	■			
Rugby Softball	43	■		■		■			
Simple Cricket	44	■		■		■			
Continuous Cricket	46	■		■		■			
Chapter 4 Attacking and Defensive Drills									
Hit and Spin Relay	49	■		■					
Hit and Spin	50	■		■					
2v1v1 Drill	51	■		■	■				
2v1+1 Drill	52	■		■	■				
Continual 3v2+2	53	■		■	■				
Breakout	54	■		■	■				
3v2 Two-Minute Drill	55	■		■	■				

(CONTINUED)

Game or Drill title	Page #	Number of players		Handling: Catching and passing	Handling: Decision making	Kicking	Defensive organization	Team attack	Team defense
		Small group	Team						
Chapter 4 Attacking and Defensive Drills *(continued)*									
4v2v2 Drill	56	■		■	■				
4v2+2 Drill	57	■		■	■				
3v5 One-Tackle Defence	58	■		■	■		■		
South-West-North-East	59	■		■	■		■		
3v4 Defence Grid	60	■		■	■		■		
2v3 Gate Defence	61	■		■	■		■		
Cover Adjustment Drill	62	■		■			■		
Cover and Chase	63	■		■	■		■		
Kick Chase Drill	64	■		■	■	■	■		
Kicking-Specific 6v6v6	65	■		■	■		■		
Chapter 5 Bag and Shield Drills									
Zigzag Runs	69	■							
Left or Right One-on-One	70	■							
Line Unity	71	■					■		
Y Drill	72	■					■		
Arc to Contact	73	■					■		
Basic Slide Drill	74	■					■		
Back and Maintain Shape	75	■					■		
Slide and Realign	76	■					■		
Bag to Shield	77	■					■		
Hit and Adjust	78	■					■		
Defensive Choice	79	■					■		
Numbered Bags	80	■	■						■
Two-Player Number Tackle	81	■	■				■		
Simultaneous Hits	82	■					■		
Up the Field	83	■	■				■		
Up, Readjust, and Cover	84	■	■				■		
Inward Adjust	85	■	■				■		
ABC Bag Drill	86	■	■				■		
Break Drill	87	■	■				■		
Realign and Defend	88	■	■	■	■		■	■	■
Live Break Drill	89		■	■	■		■	■	■
Chapter 6 Non-Specific Rugby Games									
Offside Touch	93	■		■	■				
Big Cone Touch	94	■	■	■	■				
Two-Tackle Offside Touch	95	■	■	■	■				
American Touch	96	■	■	■	■				
Kickback	98	■	■			■			
Onside Soccby	100	■	■	■	■	■	■		
Aussie Rules	101	■	■	■	■	■			
Aussie Tackle-Touch	102	■	■	■	■	■	■		

(CONTINUED)

Preface

Welcome to *Rugby Games & Drills,* a resource for rugby coaches, conditioning coaches, and teachers involved in rugby union and rugby league at all levels. This comprehensive book is packed full of ready-to-use games and drills and will help you design your own games and drills by outlining key pointers in the process. The activities in this book can be used by players of all ages and abilities; some of the simpler games that can be used with small children as major parts of a session are also suitable as part of a warm-up with adults. Many of the more complex games can and have been used to good effect with international professional players. With greater involvement, participants enjoy themselves more and are more receptive to learning, whatever their age and ability.

As a player, how many training sessions have you attended that were boring? How many hours have you spent doing mindless, repetitive drills? How much time has your field conditioning consisted of endless sprints between cones for no particular reason? How many sessions lacked any intensity during the technical and tactical part only to be followed by 10 minutes of gut-wrenching interval sprints completely unrelated to the previous hour's work?

If the preceding scenarios are familiar to you, then your coaches had little awareness of a games approach to coaching or an understanding of integrated field conditioning. This book will help you avoid falling into those traps; instead, you will create interesting, effective, and enjoyable sessions. Players of every age love to play games; this is the reason they started playing and continue to play the sport. Playing games keeps players focused and on task and physically active and develops in them a positive attitude to physical activity. The approach outlined in this book is especially useful for those who have limited time to spend with their players and must make every second count. Following is a brief explanation of what you will find in each chapter.

Chapter 1

Chapter 1 looks at the theory and practice of drills and games. It touches on theories of skill acquisition, the learning process, and games understanding.

Chapters 2 and 3

Chapters 2 and 3 look at small-sided handling and kicking games, respectively. These games can be used with any age group; some of them could be used as general games activities with children. For older players, you can use them as general skills warm-up games or as competitive but fun activities within sessions.

Chapter 4

Chapter 4, Attacking and Defensive Drills, explores ball-handling drills that aim to improve attacking play in quite closed situations. Some of these drills can also be used to develop defensive decision making. These drills were developed to improve skill in closed situations, but they can also be used as conditioning activities. The chapter explains how to adjust the number of players and conditions to get the best out of these drills.

Chapter 5

Chapter 5 is a comprehensive guide to defensive conditioning drills using bags and shields. The focus of the drills differ: some are clearly technical, and others are more purely fitness based.

Chapter 6

Chapter 6, Non-Specific Rugby Games, explores ball games derived from other sports such as Australian and American football. These are often used as fun fitness sessions in the pre-season.

Chapter 7

Chapter 7 looks into small-sided rugby-specific games. Many of these address specific aspects within a game. These games can be used within warm-ups or to address particular needs within a session, particularly as a build-up to a larger-scale game.

Chapter 8

In chapter 8, Large-Sided Rugby Games, you will learn about more demanding rugby-specific games. These games address technical and tactical requirements specific to either one or both codes of rugby. With planning, you can use these as technical and tactical development games or as a conditioning tool. In fact, with a clear, integrated approach, you can use them as both.

Chapter 9

Chapter 9, Fitness Requirements for Rugby, provides a simple and clear analysis of rugby league and rugby union. Without going into too much physiological detail, the chapter outlines the physical demands of the sports by using information from previous and current match data. From this you will begin to be able to create a picture of the necessary components of field sessions. The chapter then looks at the differences between games and drills. It looks at the uses of both of these in developing the participant as a rugby player and an athlete. You will learn how to construct drills and design games to meet the specific needs of your players and team. Once you understand this, the world will be your oyster and you will not look back.

Chapter 10

Chapter 10 addresses planning for the season, which is often a missing weapon in the coach's arsenal. Coaches often ignore the importance of progressing within a session and between sessions and constructing linked sessions throughout a training phase. Many coaching books are distant and theoretical about planning. This chapter provides a simple guide to planning your sessions based on the time of year. Finally, it provides some sample sessions using activities from within the book and explains how to construct your own.

The format for the games and drills in this book is simple and uses easy-to-understand annotated diagrams to help you follow the text. Each chapter follows a simple theme, but keep in mind that an activity may appear in one chapter and be able to be modified to fit into another. These modifications often appear in the Variations sections of games and drills. This means that although the cover of the book indicates that 119 games and drills are provided, in fact, the book contains many more. The activities can often be adapted by varying the numbers of participants or the grid size or by subtly altering the rules.

Each activity includes the following sections:

- Appropriate ages and the physical and mental components developed
- Objectives
- Equipment
- Set-up
- How to play
- Coaching points
- Variations

Appropriate Ages and Physical and Mental Components Developed

At the beginning of each game or drill, a relevant age or age range is provided. Keep in mind that this is merely a guide; early-maturing or more gifted players may be able to do more advanced drills. Likewise, beginners or players with poorer fitness may not be able to do drills designed for their age. This section also lists the physical and mental components of skill execution, decision making, speed, agility, endurance, and speed endurance. Each component is given a rating, ranging from 0 to 5, as follows:

- *0*—A rating of zero indicates that this drill or game provides very little, if any, stimulus to this physical or technical component (e.g., Zigzag Runs may have a fitness element but involves no decision-making skills by the player).
- *1*—A rating of one indicates that this drill or game provides below-average stimulation to this physical or technical component (e.g., Quick Ball Touch provides very little speed stimulus, despite its name, because the game is continuous and therefore, there is no required recovery period to enable near-maximal speed activities to take place).
- *2*—A rating of two indicates that this drill or game provides somewhat below-average stimulation to this physical or technical component (e.g., in 2 v 1 v 1, agility is rated a 2 because, whilst there is a turn at the end of the grid, the fact that there is only one defender means that there is a below-average use of "footwork" by the attacking player).
- *3*—A rating of three indicates that this drill or game provides average stimulation to this physical or technical component (e.g., in the Cover

Adjustment Drill, both speed and speed endurance are rated a 3 because speed is required to beat an opponent but never is maximal speed attained since it is a short distance; however, as the drill is repeated a number of times there is an average speed endurance component).

- ◼ *4*—A rating of four indicates that this drill or game provides above-average stimulation to this physical or technical component (e.g., in Kick Return, speed endurance is rated a 4 because there is a series of repeat kick chases carried out over quite a large distance at moderately high speeds).

- ◼ *5*—A rating of five indicates that this drill or game provides near-maximal stimulation to this physical or technical component (e.g., Pre-Exhaust the Defence provides maximal stimulation to the endurance component; however, remember to observe the correct work to rest ratios otherwise this will not occur and the score will drop).

These ratings are just a guide and alterations to an activity will affect how it stimulates the components (e.g., reducing the pitch area may increase agility and decision-making ratings; altering the number of players will alter both these components and the endurance element; changing the work-to-rest ratios will impact speed, speed endurance and endurance). And, of course, the skill and fitness levels of your players will also affect the outcome of each activity.

Objectives

Each activity lists the objective(s) it addresses. This section will help you choose activities directly geared towards your own goals for your players and the skills and components you want to address in your session.

Equipment

A simple list of equipment is included so you will know what is required to start the activity, such as how many cones you need to mark out the grids. We recommend that you have a minimum of 60 (we know 60 seems like a lot!) cones of four different colours in your stock. You should also have at least two full sets (15) of different-coloured bibs and tags and tag belts, a minimum of six tackle shields, and a similar number of tackle bags.

Set-Up

The activity set-up explains how to set up the playing area, how many players are involved on each team, and where the players are positioned at the start of the game. This will provide you with information on how the game will start and will importantly allow you to draw a map of your training session in order to help you organise it so that players can move safely and freely between activities.

How to Play

This section explains how to set up and run the activity, enabling you to easily explain it to the group. It contains the rules of the activity, which determine the particular skill and fitness component being developed.

Coaching Points

This section gives two or three points you may need to emphasize to develop your attackers and defenders. These simple cues will help the players be successful within the activity either in attack or defence.

Variations

This section provides alternative ways of running the activity. These alternatives are achieved through minor rule changes, which may affect the skill or physical component being developed.

A Note About Safety

With any coaching activity, you must carry out an adequate risk assessment. This includes checking the venue and playing surface. All cones and other rugby equipment must be checked. The players must be competent to carry out the activity you have chosen, and if they are not, you must adjust the activity accordingly. There should be an adequately trained first-aider at the venue, and you must be familiar with emergency procedures. Make sure fluid is available at all sessions; this is particularly important for younger children, who cannot efficiently control their body temperature. Encourage all players to bring their own fluid.

Also note that many of the smaller activities in this book can be used as warm-up and cool-down activities. After these activities have been used to raise the pulse and warm the muscles, some general mobility and dynamic stretching can be carried out (this is outlined in the sample sessions in chapter 10). It is important that this protocol is followed, along with some general dynamic mobility activities.

Acknowledgments

Simon Worsnop would like to thank the following coaches he has worked with in a team environment and learnt a lot from:

Gary Hetherington, Mick Cook, Gary Greinke, Phil Larder, John Kear, Steve Deakin Paul Hazelwood, Jackie Sheldon, Peter Roe, Ian Fairhurst, Andy Kelly, Richard Agar, Malcolm Reilly, Martin Hall, Matt Calland, Kevin Plant, Ken Higgins, David Waite, Brian Noble, Graham Steadman, Paul Cullen, Ray Unsworth, Brian Ashton, Damian McGrath, Jim Mallinder, Nigel Redman, Mark Mapletoft, Martin Haag, Rob Hunter, Diccon Edwards

Simon also thanks all the other coaches whom he has talked to on and off the field during his time in rugby.

City College Norwich

Customer name: MISS Sheenagh Strydom

Customer ID: 3670**

Title: Exercise physiology : nutrition, energy and human performance (7th edn.)
ID: A232664
Due: 25 Sep 2013

Title: Rugby : passing, catching, kicking.. [Know the game skills]
ID: A244344
Due: 09 Oct 2013

Title: Rugby games & drills
ID: A243771
Due: 09 Oct 2013

Title: Strength and conditioning for sport : a practical guide for coaches
ID: A244200
Due: 09 Oct 2013

Total items: 4
18/09/2013 14:01
Checked out: 4
Overdue: 0
Hold requests: 0
Ready for pickup: 0

Thank you for using the
3M SelfCheck™ System.

Key to Diagrams

○	Attacker
●	Defender
🔲	Player holding tackle shield
🎳	Player holding tackle bag
▲	Cone
⬮	Ball
→	Player movement
- - - →	Ball movement

CHAPTER 1

Using Drills and Games

technical skill involves the specific movement of a player's body to perform a particular task (e.g., passing to the left). A technical skill may break down if the player is fatigued, particularly if the player is not proficient at executing the skill (i.e., the player will revert to a previous poor skill pattern). Players must be able to repeat technical tasks as efficiently as possible (e.g., a correct pass in the 80th as well as the first minute). To make this possible, players must practise and develop skills in situations that are as close to match situations as possible, which is where the use of drills and games comes into play.

Normally, a game has a minimum of two teams and a scoring system that results in one team winning. However, in warm-up games and games with young children, the score may not be that important. In the case of drills, scoring is often not used, and the players are not necessarily in teams. However, there is a sliding continuum from drills that are strictly drills to those that may easily be changed into games right through to pure games. In addition, you can increase the pressure on players by increasing the pressure of the opponents or by having them play in a fatigued state. In this way, drills and games can be conditioning tools.

Furthermore, by incorporating skills such as small-sided games, your athletes will develop greater game sense through increased teamwork, better communication skills, and increased awareness. Also, your athletes will perform better in pressure situations during matches and develop into tactically smarter players while increasing their fitness. Finally, and probably most important, most athletes tend to enjoy skill-based conditioning more than traditional fitness conditioning methods (Coutts 2002).

Advantages and Disadvantages of Drills

Simple drills have the following advantages:

- They are easy to set up and organise in terms of numbers and equipment.
- They are easy to monitor.
- Many can be used as purely fitness activities.
- Players are unable to hide in many of them because they are quite structured and tightly-controlled.

Because of the ease of set-up and the closed nature of simple drills, they can often be combined. You can also combine them in such a way that players go from a very closed activity to progressively more open ones and finally finish with a game. For example, when concentrating on defensive decision making, you can have a group of players move progressively from a repeated static situation in which the attacking players hold shields to the same activity in which the attacking players use the ball and finally to an open modified game (see chapter 10 for more information).

You can also use drills with a fitness emphasis to exhaust players prior to a skill drill to test a particular skill under fatigue. An example of this would be to have the players do some up-and-down shuttles up a grid for one minute and then immediately go into a continuous 3v2 + 2 in which their attacking, passing, and decision-making skills are pressurised. You can combine attack and defence to test the players' ability to switch from one to the other (e.g., four players could tackle opponents, shields, or bags for a set time or number of tackles and then immediately pick up a ball and work on 4v2 + 2 for one minute). Skill drills can also be adapted to create technical and physical pressure. Using the work-to-rest principles discussed in chapter 9, you can match these drills to simple interval sessions for conditioning (e.g., repeat a combined skill drill and fitness drill sequence three times).

However, when mixing technical skill and fitness drills, you need to know whether a particular drill develops skill or fitness. In volleyball, Gabbett and colleagues (2006) found that skill-based training improves spiking, setting, and passing accuracy and spiking and passing technique, but has little effect on the physiological and anthropometric characteristics of players. However, the introduction of skill-based games provided the necessary fitness improvements. The results of this study show that skill-based conditioning games offer a specific training stimulus to simulate the physiological demands in junior elite volleyball players. Although the improvements in physical fitness after training were greater with skill-based conditioning games, instructional training resulted in greater improvements in technical skill in these athletes. These findings suggest that a combination of instructional training and skill-based conditioning games is likely to result in the greatest improvements in fitness and skill in junior elite volleyball players (Gabbett 2008).

To receive the benefits of skill-based conditioning games, athletes must perform multiple high-intensity sprint activities using sport-specific movement patterns. The intermittent nature of these games promotes the development of aerobic power as well as sport-specific speed and agility. Your role is to plan skill-based conditioning games accordingly so that the right goals are achieved in terms of rugby and fitness (see chapter 10), and to ensure that they are relevant and applicable to the age and ability of your players. Although there is a place within the field-based conditioning framework for drills, if you see players for a small amount of time each week or deal with children, you must be aware of the potential drawbacks.

Typically what happens is that the coach demonstrates the skill and then provides a large amount of instruction and correction during the drills, but teaches very little during the game. (In a recent study by the Australian Rugby League and the Australian Rugby Union, U10 coaches spent nearly half of their sessions talking!) This method has a number of drawbacks, including the following (Martens 2004):

Over-Emphasis on Technical Skills

In the traditional approach, an over-emphasis on the practice of technique is used at the expense of teaching and practising decision-making skills (i.e., game understanding) and results in drills that require no thinking and often have very little relevance to the game.

Over-Emphasis on Direct Instruction

The traditional approach relies on direct instruction which normally involves the coach telling the players what to do, rather than the players being given situations in which they must solve problems and discover the best method of success.

Away from the backyard, a novice's first introduction to sport in a club or school environment is generally through the traditional route of a purely skill-based approach of technique to cognition. A number of researchers have questioned this approach (Pill 2006). A game understanding approach, which will be discussed in more detail later, is much better for developing players who can think and act for themselves; in that way, it is also a model of player empowerment. Rather than set up an artificial 3v2 situation and tell the players in advance what attacking lines to run, you could ask the players to beat the opposition by exploring space and options, and then ask them about their successes or failures.

Mindless Factor

The traditional approach often takes the skill out of the context of the game by using a number of drills that are not related to the actual game. The principle should be, practise the way you play, and you're more likely to play the way you practised. Is tackling a tackle bag the same as tackling a nimble halfback? Is running unopposed through predetermined plays the same as running against a well-organised and reactive defence? It is one thing to practise a technique in a drill when decisions are minimal; it is quite another thing to perform it well in the pressure of a match. Technical approaches to coaching tend to develop skills out of context, whereas game-sense coaching strives to provide opportunities for learning how skills are applied in the complex and changing conditions encountered in matches (Launder 2003).

The use of rigid, structured drills with very little relevance to the game often leads to boredom, a lack of motivation, and drop-out.

Coaches studied by Richard Light in 2004 suggested that to develop player autonomy, training must place them in situations in which they are required to make decisions independent of the coach. The closer training is to the game, the more motivation there is. The further you get from the game, the less players are motivated. Actual games provide low repetition and high motivation, whereas drills offer high repetition and low motivation. Coaching via "game sense" allows for increased repetition within game contexts, which provides motivation for the players (Light 2004).

Teaching Games for Understanding Approach

The Teaching Games for Understanding Approach (TGfU) was first formally introduced by Bunker and Thorpe in the *Bulletin of Physical Education* in 1982. It has been further developed by these authors and others. In Australia and New Zealand it tends to be known as game sense, and in Rainer Martens' *Successful Coaching*, it is known as the games approach. Although all of these models have developed and evolved, they are basically describing the same approach.

In the open habit sports (team sports, combat sports and racquet sports where there are unexpected changes in situations unlike track and field events, for example), as soon as athletes know the basics of technique, the coach should constantly put them in situations that demand that they make choices and apply technique in various conditions (Drabik 1996). A player who possesses good game understanding knows where to go and how to use space and time intelligently, both alone and with team-mates, and makes decisions and takes action during a match to gain an advantage over an opposing player or team. A difference between a player who has good practical game understanding and a player who has tactical knowledge is that the former can make the correct decision within a match situation, whereas the latter may have the appropriate knowledge but be unable to apply it. This ability to make tactical decisions can be termed *game understanding*. This tactical ability is not the same as strategy, which is the plan of action for the team or the so-called game plan.

Many great players do appear to have the intuitive ability to do the right thing at the right time, and it is conceivable that a genetic element is involved. However, we believe that intuition is simply the distilled essence of prior experience and has usually been developed through endless pick-up games and informal practices (Launder 2003). Playing the game gives meaning to their performance and actively involves them in the learning process. By involving learners in games and in the decision-making process required to play games, you can encourage both game appreciation and physical skill development (Griffen and Butler 2005). The students learn the 'what to do' before the 'how to do.'

Coaches often spend a great deal of time teaching technique, but not much time teaching aspects such as decision making, risk, deception, spatial awareness, understanding and counteracting an opponent, and recognising scoring opportunities. Traditionally, coaching has been very technique based. Although this may be appropriate for some of the more closed skill sports, in other sports, technique is over-emphasised. This traditional technical approach begins with the question, How is this skill performed?, and then focuses on teaching the skills of the game before putting the skills into practice. It conditions participants to pay attention to technique during the activity and not the joy of being active. It emphasises correcting movement patterns rather than enhancing them. Unfortunately, the result is that most beginners cannot perform the complex skills necessary for success (Pill 2006).

These days, children and newcomers to a sport are often familiar with the whole games approach, unlike their predecessors 30 or 40 years ago, which has implications for the methods and styles of coaching. Kirk and MacPhail (2002) suggested that saturation of elite-level sport through the mass media has resulted in children having an expectation of what the game will feel like to play. They argued that a traditional, prescribed-drills approach is unlikely to meet that expectation. They suggested that a TGfU introduction is more likely to provide newcomers with an initial feel of the game that fits with their expectations and motivates them for further participation (Slade 2007).

Clearly, it is important to play games! Games are needed that challenge players at every level and enhance their ability to react quickly and make decisions. This is particularly relevant to working with children because they want to play games, not practise drills, many of which they do not understand. Play makes them aware of the role of particular techniques in the game and motivates them to do drills when the time comes. Remember that children join a team because they want to play the sport, not because they want to drill (Drabik 1996).

The TGfU model revolves around the use of key questions to guide the players' understanding of the conceptual, strategic, and tactical requirements of the game, combined with game modifications that allow players to learn the game without having to pay excessive attention to technique (Pill 2006).

Rather than having lines of children who are waiting to go through a skill drill, you can have all children actively playing the game they love. Introduce skills during the game, and use small-sided games to maximise participation. Most important, shift from thinking about the skills of the game to thinking about the nature of the game. Use a game-question-reflect-practise cycle rather than the traditional practise-instruct-practise-culminating game cycle (Pill 2006).

In essence, the TGfU model reverses the traditional order of teaching games by having students learn about the game and practise the technique within the context of the game rather than separate from it. The game and its tactics are central to the lesson or practice, rather than tagged on at the end or left for extra-curricular practice time. The TGfU approach first teaches players what the game is about. In contrast to the highly structured coach-centred approach, it is a player-centred journey of discovery. Games can be used to develop technical skills, decision-making abilities, and fitness. The use of games has a proven track record across a wide variety of sports. For example, esteemed Australian hockey coach Ric Charlesworth (1999) had this to say regarding the approach:

> A variety of possibilities can establish an interesting training environment which economically uses the time available. Designer games are in my view one of the best. Any number of training drills can emphasise skills and/or provide physically taxing tasks. However, few offer the continuity of the designer game and none provide the competitive, strategic, distracted and 'decision laden' environment in which to do it. That is why these situations are found to be challenging and fun by players. Many comment that it's almost 'not like hockey training.'

The TGfU method is not ad hoc (i.e., simply letting the players play). The original TGfU model developed by Bunker and Thorpe in 1982 involved the following steps (Griffen and Butler 2005):

- *Step 1:* A game is introduced that is appropriate to the players.
- *Step 2:* The players are made aware of rules, scoring, boundaries, and so on.
- *Step 3:* Tactical awareness is introduced via the game.
- *Step 4:* To make appropriate decisions, students must focus on the decision-making processes in games.
- *Step 5:* Skill execution is viewed within the context of the game.
- *Step 6:* Performance is judged on the specific criteria of that game, session, or block.

Several years later, Thorpe and Bunker (1989) introduced four pedagogical principles associated with the TGfU approach:

- *Games sampling,* which explores similarities among various games.
- *Representation,* which involves playing a condensed game that represents the essence of the sport (in our case, rugby) as a whole.
- *Exaggeration,* which requires making changes to the rules, the pitch, and so on, to highlight a specific tactical problem.
- *Tactical complexity,* which requires the coach to match the game to the age and playing standards of the players.

To design appropriate games, you must understand the following three key planning steps:

1. Understanding the basic structure of the game

The basic structure of the game has to do with the skill or tactic you want to develop. Is your goal to develop fitness or mental skills? You should have a clear aim for the game and the session and the part the game plays within that session. If you are working with young children, your goal may also be to develop cognitive development, cooperation, and self-worth. Always be clear about the use of space, equipment, numbers, and movements, as well as the rules and how subtle changes to them will affect the outcome of the game. Make sure you have a clear picture of the following:

- Time
- Number of players
- Pitch size
- Method(s) of scoring
- Passing rules
- Contact and recycling rules
- Tackle number

2. Modifying the basic game structure

Begin by choosing a game you are familiar with and modify one basic component; then modify another component in the next session, and continue progressively in this way, creating linked sessions. For example, with less skilled players, you could use a game such as Keep Ball and overload the attack in a larger grid by using seven attackers against three defenders in a 20-by-20-metre grid. You could then progressively work towards 5v5 in a 12-by-12-metre grid as the players improve.

3. Managing the difficulty of the game

You need to recognise your players' particular skill limitations and areas in which they can improve. Create progressive plans, and understand the limits to development within a particular time frame.

Once you have decided on the game and the goals of the session, you can use the TGfU model to break the session down into four parts, or components.

- *Game form:* The initial game will normally be a version of the full game. It will typically include two essential characteristics: representation and exaggeration, meaning that it will represent the game in a modified form but may exaggerate one particular rule to emphasise a particular tactical aspect (e.g., 6v4 rotation to exploit space).
- *Game-related practice:* If a particular tactical part was badly exploited (e.g., players failed to exploit 2v1 or 3v2 overlaps on the outside), players could now practise this in a drill.
- *Skill practice (technical focus), if required:* If the 2v1 broke down because players could not pass accurately, they could then practise passing as an isolated skill.
- *Modified or full game:* Players now return to the original game, or a modification of it (e.g., Touch Overload on page 121 or Base Cone Touch on page 139).

This method of teaching a skill within a game and then practising it as a drill before returning to a game is known as the whole-part-whole method. Begin by explaining the rules and presenting a few basic techniques without detailed descriptions (just enough to give a rough idea of what to do), and then let the athletes play. 'After the play, point out the separate skills or techniques that the athletes used and teach these skills one by one; then apply them again in action. Stress the application of newly learned skills in realistic conditions' (Drabik 1996).

The exaggeration of the rules described by Thorpe and Bunker and the coaching you do within the session are vital for this approach to succeed. If the game is primarily intended to enhance physical fitness, then it will be familiar to the players who should have a good competence set, so that intensity is not compromised by skill breakdown. Martens (2004) suggested three methods for modifying the game using the TGfU, or games, approach: shaping play, focusing play, and enhancing play.

Shaping Play

Similar to Thorpe and Bunker's principle of exaggeration, shaping play involves teaching the players through the medium of a game that has been shaped to suit the purpose of the session. By changing certain aspects of the game, you can create a variety of learning situations. Following are some options:

- Alter the rules of the game (e.g., the number of tackles, an introduction of a forward pass, the number of passes allowed, the time allowed in possession).
- Adjust the number of players on the attack or defence, or both.
- Alter the size of the field or grid to increase or decrease space (e.g., alter the positioning of the goalposts or goal line, or use more than one set of goalposts per team).
- Alter the method of scoring (e.g., introduce penalty or bonus points for particular plays).

The key in shaping play is to design the game so that your athletes have the opportunity to practise what is relevant in the real game and are practising according to the particular theme and aim of the session.

Focusing Play

You cannot just shape the game and hope the players teach themselves; therefore, it is important to focus the attention of the players on the key elements within the modified game and how to succeed (tactical awareness). Within this decision-making environment, question the players about the situations that have arisen and their responses to them. The games can be quite simple or more complicated (i.e., work to develop quite technical aspects of play). This is where you must work with your conditioner, if you have one, so that both the physical and technical or tactical aims of the session are met.

Enhancing Play

Enhancing play can involve challenging your players by creating demanding situations (e.g., the team is repeatedly penalised, it is the last five minutes, and the team is a targeted number of points behind). In the TGfU approach, the practice is focused on developing the player, whereas in the traditional approach, the practice is focused on obeying the coach. Therefore, the TGfU approach moves from a coach-centred model to a player-centred model. 'One of the most striking findings of Butler's 1993 study was that, although many teachers believed that they used a child-centred approach, in reality they taught using a directive approach' (Griffen and Butler 2005).

Many people wonder whether the games approach develops skill as efficiently as a traditional approach does. Rugby field-based training is normally aimed at improving the technical and tactical parts of the team's performance. The sessions can concentrate on individual skills, group skills, or more tactical team play. Individual skills can be closed, such as kicking a set distance or passing accurately over a specific distance, or they can be more open, involving decision making (e.g., beating a defender in a 2v1 situation). Technical skills and decision making have been improved in a number of ways.

A skill is said to have been learnt if there is a relatively permanent improvement in the performance of that skill as a result of practice. In the past, it was thought that sporting experts learned technical skills by developing mental blueprints as a result of repeating simple tasks. However, even quite simple tasks consist of many responses of a similar type, especially in an open situation in which team-mates and opponents provide the player with decisions to make. It is now thought that top players take out key pieces of information every time they practise to create new rules for the future. Therefore, it is important to provide players with opportunities to develop their decision-making skills in open situations during practice.

Coaching Using the TGfU Method

The ability to teach technical skills in a positive and productive manner is vital for the continued interest in and participation of people in rugby. This kind of coaching will lead to an improvement in technical ability (and hence self-worth) and the success of the individual player and the team.

The main ways you teach skills are verbally or visually (by demonstration), or a combination of both. A demonstration is most effective for a simple closed skill with a particular movement; it may be less useful for refining an existing skill. Unless success depends on the perfect execution of one form of a skill, verbal instruction may be more effective. Equal emphasis should be placed on the demonstration and its desired outcome so that performers can find their own routes to efficiency. Evidence has shown that performers should focus largely on the desired effects of the skill (i.e., goal-focused instruction) rather than on the skill itself (i.e., form-based instruction). This means focusing on the delivery of the pass rather than on each individual coaching point. The focus on the goal rather than on the action itself encourages players to find their own methods of success.

Following the instruction or demonstration, you must decide how best to structure the session to help players improve the skill(s) you are addressing. You may be familiar with the following methods of practice and may even have used them all.

■ *Massed practice*. Massed practice involves repeating a skill over and over within a closed drill. This type of practice is common in the traditional approach and can lead to fatigue and boredom, particularly in people with short concentration spans (e.g., younger players).

- *Distributive practice*. Distributive practice involves breaking the skill into smaller sections throughout the session. Recent research suggests that distributive practice is better than massed practice for both performance and learning.
- *Blocked practice*. Blocked practice involves practising a particular skill continuously the same way within a session (e.g., a scrum half passing from the floor left to right over the same distance from the same starting position).
- *Random practice*. Random practice involves practising the skill in slightly different situations (e.g., passing the ball from different directions, from different heights, for different distances, or from different starting positions or interspersing the pass with other similar skills).

Should players practise skills as a block or randomly mixed with other skills? Most research shows that skills are most readily acquired in the short term from blocked practice. Practice schedules that involve blocked, massed, and constant practice of a single skill result in better performance of the skill during that particular practice. Thorpe stated that 'Research into massed/distributed, constant/random (i.e., skill acquisition theory) would suggest this (approach) is not appropriate to learning' (Kidman 2001). Blocked practice has been traditionally used in a lot of sports, probably because, as Thorpe stated earlier, '. . . Perhaps outweighing all other points is that the prescriptive approach produced quick 'performance' changes within the lesson. Remember that people judged the success of their coaching on the session "I think that went well." The coaches seem to grasp that. The same people would be found the following session or, after the next game, to be complaining that the players had forgotten everything: "Don't you remember what we did?" Of course they didn't [remember] because we taught for rapid performance change not for deep-rooted learning.'

Considerable evidence suggests strong benefits from more variable and random practice and stronger retention of a skill as a result of random practice. Sessions that encourage variable, distributed, and random practice of multiple skills promote more effective learning in the medium to long term than blocked practice. Instructional training resulted in considerable improvements in technique accuracy in all tasks. However, skill-based conditioning games resulted in few improvements in technical skill and accuracy.

These findings differ, at least partially, from those of others, who reported greater improvements in passing skill execution, but not accuracy, in hockey players who trained with small-sided games in comparison to technical instruction. It has been suggested that that technical instruction that encompasses blocked practice provides greater short-term improvements in skill than random practice does. However, longer-term performance benefits are greater in those who use random practice (Gabbett 2008).

These finding support the use of games interspersed with skill drills to improve technical and tactical performance (i.e., the whole-part-whole method). This approach can be used by sandwiching a skill drill between physically demanding games as a recovery, or by sandwiching a tough closed drill between less physically demanding games. The combinations will depend on the aims of the session and the demands of each activity.

The ability to challenge and encourage players to work outside their comfort zones is a characteristic of a good coach. As a coach, you should challenge yourself by continually re-evaluating your coaching philosophy, your coaching methods, and your communication style (Gabbett 2001). Good coaches do far more than just present technical and tactical knowledge; they give players a real understanding of the sport. They do this by giving players opportunities to make intelligent decisions and by encouraging self-reflection. With better understanding and increased autonomy, players can take greater responsibility for their own learning. 'Knowledge acquired on one's own by creative trial and error is better assimilated and more permanent than knowledge served ready-made' (Drabik 1996).

To be successful in using the TGfU approach, outline a coaching section (rugby sections would typically be offence, defence, and kicking) and then a topic and aims within that section (see figure 1.1). Then, create a game to develop the section. In this figure the coaching section is offence, and it is broken down further into the section topic (non-contact offence) and the aims of this section topic (good grip and passing accuracy, support play and decision making, and attacking shape and options).

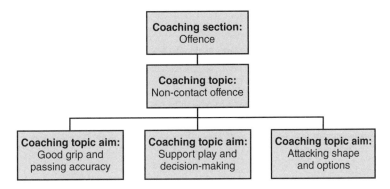

Figure 1.1.   Sample coaching section, topic, and aims.

After determining your coaching section, topic, and aims, develop a game in which players can practise these aims. For example, say you have a group of 14-year-old players and a 15-by-15-metre grid for warm-up. How could you alter a simple game of Keep Ball (page 24) to provide an endless supply of variations to improve passing accuracy and a good palmless grip on the ball? See table 1.1 for some ideas. The various combinations of handling and conditioning rules provide potentially over 40 variations!

This simple alteration of basic skills or conditioning dimensions can be applied to a whole range of games. Table 1.2 shows the various coaching aims that can be applied to a game for a variety of topics.

You can develop many small- or large-sided games to work on these particular aims. When developing the games, be sure that you understand how the rules of the game will affect the outcome of the game. Not paying enough attention to details when designing games could cause them to have different physiological or technical outcomes than those you aimed for. For example, you could design a game to help a team improve its attacking shape, but if the number of players or the speed of the breakdown is altered, then

TABLE 1.1 Possible Variations for Keep Ball

Game	Keep Ball
Description	Have players play 4v4 in a 15-by-15-metre grid. One group must try to put together 10 passes to score one point. All players can move. No contact is permitted.
Skill emphasis	Catch, grip, carry
Conditioning emphasis	Improving agility and the ability to make decisions quickly; endurance element introduced if played for longer than 30 seconds.
Variations	**Skill variations** • Two-handed pass, carry or catch • One-handed pass, carry or catch • One- or two-handed pass to the left or right only • Overhead pass only, using one or two hands • Bounce pass only, using one or two hands • Show and retract before passing using one hand • Introduce a kick to the sequence **Conditioning variations** • The ball carrier may not move. • The ball carrier may not move and must pass the ball within five seconds. • After passing the ball, the player must touch a corner cone. • After passing the ball, the player must drop to the floor. • Introduce player-on-player marking. • Give the defending team tackle shields and allow contact. • Vary the total number of players, duration, or both. • Overload the defence or attack.
Implications of variations	• They introduce technical and concentration differences. • The ball carrier and players off the ball must work harder and think faster. • The ball carrier must overcome body weight. • Players must use agility to stay with opponents. • The ball carrier and catcher must work to stay on their feet using strength and balance.

the focus of the game will be lost (e.g., in the case of attacking shape, if the speed of the breakdown is too quick, the support players will not be able to get in position; if the numbers are too low, there will not be enough players to act as support runners; if the defence has reduced numbers, the offence will achieve success via fast hands and exploiting space rather than the use of attacking shape and good options).

Using conditioned games for fitness has been shown to be not only more interesting to the players and more beneficial to their development, but also be less injurious than traditional conditioning methods. The majority of injuries (90.9 per 1,000 training hours, or 37.5 percent) were sustained during traditional conditioning activities that involved no skill component (e.g., running without the ball). In contrast, the incidence of injuries sustained while participating in skill-based conditioning games was low (26.0 per 1,000 training hours, or 10.7 percent; Gabbett 2002).

TABLE 1.2	Coaching Topics and Possible Coaching Aims
Coaching topic	**Coaching aims**
Handling	• Grip and carry • Support and decision making • Attacking shape and options • Attacking from set piece
Kicking	• Simple kicking and catching skills • Kick to score • Defensive kicking • Offensive kicking • Kick chase • Counterattack • Restart • Drop goal
Defence	• Individual, two, or three-person tackle technique • Play the ball, or ruck defence • Line defence • Defensive organisation from a set piece • Defensive organisation in phase play against various numbers • On-line defence
Breakdown	• Play-the-ball (league) • Ruck, maul, recycling (union) • Body position • Grappling and floor work
Set piece (union)	• Lineout • Scrum

When conducting a conditioning session with a previous England U21 team, a player approached the coach and said that he had a hamstring 'tweak' and would not be able to participate. When the coach told him that the conditioning would be the 6v4 rotation game, the player reported that he would be fine. What he meant was that he did not feel like doing repeat sprints! In fact, the player worked harder in the games than he would have done in repeat sprints and suffered no ill effects. 'It is possible that players were less likely to report transient injuries sustained while performing skill-based conditioning games, because they found this form of physical conditioning more challenging and enjoyable than traditional conditioning activities. Because of the high motivation of the rugby league players in the present study, these possibilities appear unlikely' (Gabbett 2002).

Regardless of the explanation for the lower injury rates during skill-based conditioning games, results demonstrate that significantly less training time is lost to injuries sustained in these activities (Gabbett 2002). I have found virtually no occurrence of non-contact soft tissue injury when using themed games as a method of physical conditioning in the last 10 years. This fact corroborates with evidence that shows that conditioning activities that have no skill component (e.g., high-volume running activities) are traditionally associated with a high incidence of overuse injuries (Brukner and Khan 1994).

The intensity and volume of games are easy to modify to suit the physical needs of players; this is particularly true when sessions are physiologically monitored (e.g., if players are tired, the physical demands of the game can easily be reduced by shortening the playing area, which will reduce the distance the ball needs to be kicked or the distance players need to sprint). These results suggest that this type of training may reduce injury rates at training. The potential for injury during these games can be decreased by rule or equipment modifications. In particular, minimising unnecessary body contact and collisions and increasing the amount of protective clothing may assist with this. Furthermore, implementing skill-based games that involve physical contact at the start of a training sessions when athletes are fresh may further reduce the risk of injury (Coutts 2002).

Using a games approach appears to be a win–win situation. The players are motivated to play and are intrinsically motivated to work harder, and at the same time they are improving their skills and decision making in game-related practice. Now that we have addressed the advantages of using games, how to adapt them to particular players and teams, and the various ways to include skill drills within the overall practice, we will look at specific games and drills to develop your players.

Small-Sided Handling Games

The small-sided handling games in this chapter are for a small number of players, usually eight or fewer per group, and tend to concentrate on the basic skills of grip, carry, catch, and passing accuracy. The games also encourage communication and support play. They are suitable as warm-up games for adults and as main games for younger and less experienced players.

All players should be able to pass the ball accurately to the left and right while standing or running. Players should be able to adjust the strength of their pass based on the distance to the player receiving the ball. Players should also become adept at passing with a single hand in a number of directions and at a variety of angles. Catching and passing are fundamental sport skills and should form part of the basic sport literacy programme of all young rugby players. Rugby is a late specialisation sport, and therefore, all players should have adequate short and long passing skills in both directions before they start to concentrate on individual position-specific skills. It is important that children use a ball that is the correct size so that they can carry out these key skills.

The games at the beginning of the chapter, such as Running Tag, Rob the Nest, Rob the Den, and Circle Dodge Ball, are designed to promote maintaining a good grip on the ball and delivering an accurate pass; however, they do not require a great deal of decision making. They are similar to simple relays except that they are more fun and involve more game-specific agility. These simple games can be introduced to very young children to familiarise them with the basics of carrying the ball and can be used as part of a varied session involving the coaching of grip and carry technique.

The next two games, Air Catch and Lift and Catch, are designed to test aerial catching skills, the second in a rugby union–specific context. Aerial catching skills are a vital part of many team sports and become increasingly important in rugby as players develop kicking skills and tactics. Often, aerial skills are taught in isolation with repetitive drills. Although such drills have their place, it is important to introduce a fun and competitive element to make them more interesting, and you can do this very easily.

Once players are able to pass and catch with reasonable accuracy, they need to further develop their skills. This can be done with the small-sided games in this chapter, in which they practise passing accuracy in a competitive but enjoyable way. Small-sided games also require players to work as a team (thus encouraging communication and teamwork), to maintain possession of the ball under pressure from their opponents, or to catch and tag their opponents with the ball. All of these games reward the basic core skills of passing accurately, catching quickly, and passing the ball on at pace. The players will have to make decisions as to who to pass to based on the available space around them, their team-mates, and their opponents.

Finally, Hit the Cone on page 29 and the games that follow it are invasion games. Apart from the final activity, Channel Ball on page 34, passing in any direction is allowed. This not only develops spatial awareness in a 360-degree view around each player, but also allows young children and players with less ability to enjoy games that enhance their rugby skills without having to learn the more difficult skill of passing backwards accurately at pace.

Note that only two of the games, the Keep Ball Contact Variation (page 26) and Channel Ball (page 34), involve contact, but you can add varying amounts of contact to many of the games once your players have achieved competence. Remember what the core aim of the activity is, however; if the addition of any increased pressure through contact causes a large breakdown in skill, then give it up.

RUNNING TAG

AGES: ALL

Skill execution: 1 ● Decision making: 0 ● Speed: 1

Agility: 5 ● Endurance: 2 ● Speed endurance: 2

OBJECTIVES
To learn how to change direction quickly to chase other players and to hold the ball correctly.

EQUIPMENT
Up to eight balls, four cones

SET-UP
Mark out a 5-by-5-metre to 20-by-20-metre grid with cones, depending on the age, number, and skill level of the players. Split 8 to 16 players into two equal teams. Give a ball to up to half the players.

HOW TO PLAY
The players with rugby balls hold them in two hands and chase the players not carrying balls, attempting to tag them with the balls they are carrying. Players who are tagged leave the grid. Time how long each team takes to tag all the players, or see how many players are tagged in a given time in order to determine a winner.

COACHING POINTS
- Players should hold and run with the ball correctly.
- Players should attempt to evade other players.

VARIATION
Instead of leaving the grid, the tagged players stay in the grid and can be released by members of their own team (e.g., by being jumped over in a squat position or by a team member crawling through the player's legs).

ROB THE NEST

AGES: ALL

Skill execution: 1 ● Decision making: 1 ● Speed: 2

Agility: 4 ● Endurance: 2 ● Speed endurance: 2

OBJECTIVE

To learn how to change direction quickly to pick up and put down a stationary ball.

EQUIPMENT

Up to eight balls, four cones

SET-UP

Mark out a 5-by-5-metre to 10-by-10-metre grid with cones, depending on the age and skill level of the players. Split 8 to 16 players into four equal teams. The players stand outside the grid at their team's cone. Place six to eight balls in the centre of the grid.

HOW TO PLAY

On your command, the first player in each line enters the grid and takes one ball at a time and places it outside the grid by their cone. Once the balls from the centre have gone, the players can steal balls from the other teams' cones. The game stops when one team has three or four balls at their cone. The game restarts with the balls placed back in the centre of the grid and the next player in line at the cone, ready to enter.

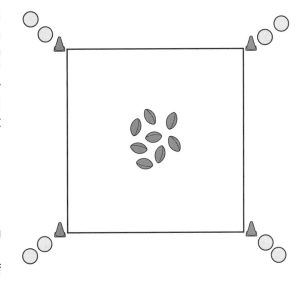

COACHING POINTS

- Players should pick balls up correctly.
- Players should attempt to evade other players.
- Players should hold the ball in two hands when running.
- Players should place the balls down carefully as if scoring a try.

ROB THE DEN

AGES: ALL

Skill execution: 1 ● **Decision making: 1** ● **Speed: 1**

Agility: 3 ● **Endurance: 2** ● **Speed endurance: 2**

OBJECTIVES

To learn evasion skills and how to pick up a stationary ball.

EQUIPMENT

Up to ten balls, six cones

SET-UP

Mark out a circle with cones with a radius of 3 to 5 metres depending on the age and skill level of the players. Inside the circle is a central den that contains up to 10 balls. Split 8 to 16 players into four equal teams. One team is inside the circle; the other teams are outside.

HOW TO PLAY

The game starts on your command. The players outside the circle attempt to run in and steal a ball and take it outside the circle. Players inside the circle are defenders attempting to keep outside players from stealing balls. A player stealing the ball who is touched by a player inside the circle must put the ball back inside the central den and becomes a defender inside the circle. The last player left on the outside is the winner.

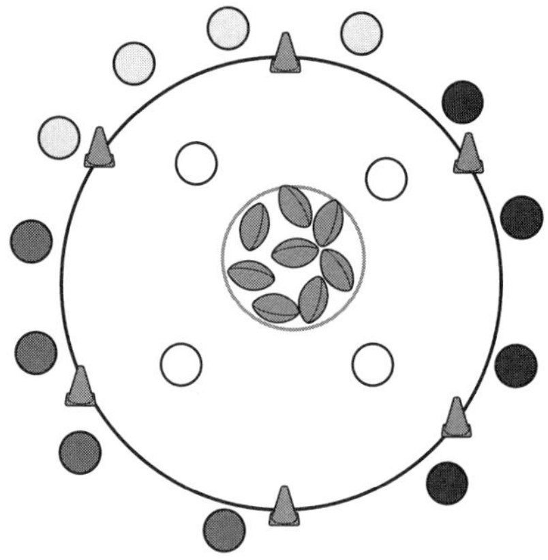

COACHING POINTS

- Players should pick balls up correctly.
- Players should attempt to evade other players.
- Players should hold the ball in two hands.

VARIATIONS

The touch must be two-handed between the waist and shoulder; the players inside the circle must complete full tackles on the robbers; the player who makes the tackle must tackle and then unload and compete for the ball in the appropriate manner.

CIRCLE DODGE BALL

AGES: ALL

Skill execution: 1 • Decision making: 0 • Speed: 0

Agility: 2 • Endurance: 0 • Speed endurance: 0

OBJECTIVE
To develop accuracy in the pass.

EQUIPMENT
Up to three balls, six cones

SET-UP
Mark out a circle with cones with a radius of 3 to 5 metres depending on the age and skill level of the players. Split 12 players into three teams of four players. One team is inside the circle, and the other teams are outside. One player from each team outside the circle has a ball.

HOW TO PLAY
On your command, the players outside the circle pass the balls at the players inside the circle, attempting to hit them. Count the number of hits within a set period of time to determine the winner. This game can also be played by having players who have been hit leave the circle; the last player left in the circle wins. Players outside the grid may enter the circle to collect balls.

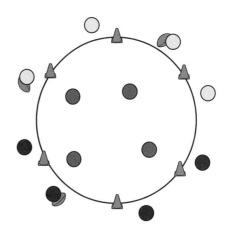

COACHING POINTS
- Players should make accurately weighted passes.
- Players inside the circle should maintain good agility and evasion techniques.

VARIATIONS
Introduce more balls; count only passes that hit players between the waist and chest; expand the circle to more than 10 metres in diameter and have players use grubber kicks, allowing only strikes below the waist.

AIR CATCH

AGES: ALL

Skill execution: 2 • Decision making: 0 • Speed: 0

Agility: 2 • Endurance: 0 • Speed endurance: 0

OBJECTIVES

To develop basic high catching and jumping skills.

EQUIPMENT

One ball, four cones

SET-UP

Mark out a 20-by-20-metre grid with cones. Split 4 to 16 players into two equal groups. One player from each team is given a number and is paired up with a player from the other team who has the same number.

HOW TO PLAY

The game starts with the coach throwing the ball into the air and calling a number. Upon hearing the call, the pair of players with this number run, jump, and compete for the ball. The player who successfully catches the ball now has the opportunity to throw the ball and call a new number. If neither member of the pair catches the ball, throw the ball up for one member of the pair to catch to restart the game.

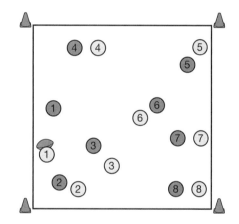

COACHING POINTS

- Players should keep their eyes on the ball.
- Players should put their hands up with fingers spread to catch the ball.
- Players should execute a jump off the forward leg and should be able to do this off both legs.

VARIATION

Introduce more balls into the game, at increasingly shorter intervals.

LIFT AND CATCH

AGES: 15+

Skill execution: 3 ● Decision making: 0 ● Speed: 0

Agility: 3 ● Endurance: 0 ● Speed endurance: 1

OBJECTIVES

To develop accurate lineout and kick-off catching, lifting, and jumping skills.

EQUIPMENT

Three balls, four cones

SET-UP

Mark out a 10-by-20-metre to 20-by-30-metre grid with cones, depending on the age and skill level of the players. Split 18 players into two teams of nine players, and then split each team further into groups of three. Each group of three from one team has a ball.

HOW TO PLAY

The groups with a ball throw it up in the air to the opposing groups, who catch the ball using lifting pod skills. A team scores a point for each successful catch. Teams alternate between throwing and catching. The first team to score ten points is the winner.

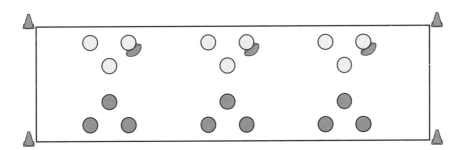

COACHING POINTS

- Lifting players must maintain strong backs and lift the catchers straight up.
- Catching players must raise their arms and spread their fingers.
- Catching player must maintain a strong core and stay straight up.

VARIATIONS

Mix the pods throughout the grid rather than positioning them in two lines; have players use kicks rather than throws; make each pod an individual team; allow the team that has thrown or kicked the ball to run and challenge (legally) for possession.

KEEP BALL

AGES: ALL

Skill execution: 3 ● Decision making: 3 ● Speed: 1

Agility: 4 ● Endurance: 3 ● Speed endurance: 1

OBJECTIVES

To learn how to make correct decisions and accurate passes under pressure.

EQUIPMENT

One ball, four cones

SET-UP

Mark out a 5-by-5-metre to 20-by-20-metre grid with cones, depending on the age and skill level of the players. Split 4 to 12 players into two equal teams.

HOW TO PLAY

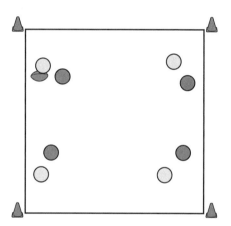

Pass the ball to a player on one team. This player is not allowed to move with the ball and must pass to another member of the team, trying to keep it from being intercepted by a player on the other team. All players except the ball carrier may move. The players on the team without the ball may not interfere with the other team's players; they must only attempt to go for the ball. Only rugby passes are allowed. Once a team with the ball has achieved a number of passes (e.g., 10), it scores a point and the other team starts with the ball.

COACHING POINTS

- Players should make accurately weighted passes.
- Players should use good agility and evasion techniques.
- Players should strive for good off-the-ball running and exploitation of space.

VARIATIONS

Make the grid larger; after passing the ball, a player must touch the corner cone or go to the ground at the corner cone before being alive again; the ball carrier is allowed to move with the ball for a specific time or number of steps; reduce the number of players to two on each side to increase the demand; have advanced players use left-hand, right-hand, overhead passing; use a 20-by-20-metre grid and introduce a kick.

KEEP BALL VARIATION

AGES: 11+

Skill execution: 3 ● **Decision making: 3** ● **Speed: 2**

Agility: 2 ● **Endurance: 3** ● **Speed endurance: 2**

OBJECTIVES

To learn how to make correct decisions and accurate passes under pressure.

EQUIPMENT

One ball, four cones

SET-UP

Mark out a 10-by-10-metre to 30-by-30-metre grid with cones, depending on the age and skill level of the players. Split 16 players into two equal teams. Four players from each team begin inside the grid; the remaining four from each team are on the four sidelines.

HOW TO PLAY

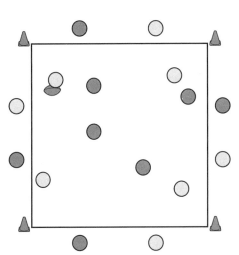

Pass the ball to a player on one team. This player is not allowed to move with the ball and must pass to another member of the team, trying to keep it from being intercepted by a player on the other team. In this variation, the player who has the ball now has a choice of passing to a team-mate within the grid or to a team-mate just outside the grid. The players on the outside of the grid may not move or pass to each other. Interference between players on opposing teams inside or outside the grid is not allowed. Once a team with the ball has achieved a number of passes (e.g., 10), it scores a point and the other team starts with the ball.

COACHING POINTS

- Player should make accurately weighted passes.
- Players should use good agility and evasion techniques.
- Players should strive for good off-the-ball running and exploitation of space.

VARIATIONS

The ball carrier is allowed to move with the ball; the outside players are allowed to move up and down their side of the grid; the team with the ball may be touched by the opponents only a certain number of times (e.g., three) before having to turn the ball over; the defending team is allowed to grip the ball carrier in an attempt to steal the ball or to create a fumble; players use a player-on-player marking system in which each player is assigned a specific opponent; players may use only specific passes or kicks.

KEEP BALL CONTACT VARIATION

AGES: 12+

Skill execution: 3 ● Decision making: 3 ● Speed: 1

Agility: 3 ● Endurance: 3 ● Speed endurance: 1

OBJECTIVES

To learn how to make correct decisions and accurate passes under pressure and contact; to improve proficiency in the avoidance of collision.

EQUIPMENT

One ball, four cones, tackle shields for half of the players

SET-UP

Mark out a 10-by-10-metre to 20-by-20-metre grid with cones, depending on the age and skill level of the players. Split 8 to 12 players into two equal teams. One team has tackle shields.

HOW TO PLAY

Pass the ball to a player on the team without tackle shields. This player is not allowed to move with the ball and must pass to another member of the team, trying to keep it from being intercepted by a player on the other team. In this variation, players on the team with the ball are under pressure from those on the opposing team, who are aiming to knock them over or knock them out of the grid. The ball carrier should try to avoid contact, but when it occurs, must be strong. Once the team with the ball has achieved a number of passes (e.g., 10), it scores a point and the other team starts with the ball.

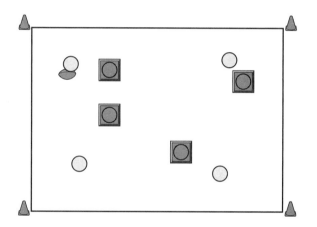

COACHING POINTS

- Players should make accurately weighted passes.
- Players should use good agility and evasion techniques.
- Players should strive for good off-the-ball running and exploitation of space.
- Players should use strong skills in contact.

VARIATIONS

Require specific contact situations of the ball carrier before the ball is passed (e.g., hit and spin, bump off, bust through, stand and drive with support, support player to enter and rip the ball); with a larger number of players per team, have two players support the ball carrier who is making contact with a shield, to clear the nearest threats.

BALL TAG

AGES: ALL

Skill execution: 3 ● Decision making 2 ● Speed: 1

Agility: 3 ● Endurance: 2 ● Speed endurance: 1

OBJECTIVES

To develop accurate passing and good decision making and team communication; to improve agility.

EQUIPMENT

One ball, four cones

SET-UP

Mark out a 10-by-10-metre to 20-by-20-metre grid with cones, depending on the age and skill level of the players. Split 8 to 12 players into two equal teams.

HOW TO PLAY

To begin, pass the ball; the team that catches the ball becomes the tagging team. The player with the ball may not move. The team in possession must touch an opponent with the ball (this is typically done by working an opponent into a corner using quick passes). Players who are tagged are out of the game. Once the tagging team tags all of the opponents, teams switch. The team that tags players in the shortest amount of time is the winner. The winner can also be determined based on how many players are tagged in a specific amount of time.

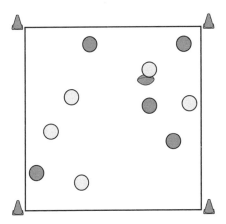

COACHING POINTS

- Players should make accurately weighted passes.
- Players on the team without the ball should use good agility and evasion techniques.

VARIATIONS

Tagged players stands with their legs apart and are brought back into the game by a team-mate crawling through their legs; start with uneven numbers (e.g., three ball carriers and six on the chased team), and members of the chased team who are caught must join the ball carriers.

FIFTH COLUMNIST

AGES: ALL

Skill execution: 3 ● Decision making: 2 ● Speed: 0

Agility: 2 ● Endurance: 1 ● Speed endurance: 0

OBJECTIVES

To learn how to make correct decisions and accurate passes.

EQUIPMENT

One ball, four cones

SET-UP

Mark out a 10-by-15-metre to 20-by-30-metre grid with cones, depending on the age and skill level of the players. Mark a centre line on the grid. Split 12 players into two equal teams. Five players from each team are in half of the grid, and the sixth player is in the opponents' half.

HOW TO PLAY

The game starts when you throw the ball into the grid. The team that catches the ball then attempts to get the ball to its fifth columnist (i.e., the player who is in the other half of the grid) to score a point. The players may not run with the ball but may pass it in any direction. If the ball is intercepted, the players on the other team should immediately try to pass to their fifth columnist. If the ball is dropped or passed inaccurately, but not intercepted, the other team gains possession of the ball, and you restart play behind their end line. The game is played for a set period of time. To begin, only rugby passes are allowed.

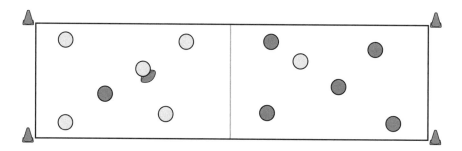

COACHING POINTS

- Players should make accurately weighted passes.
- The fifth columnists should use good agility and evasion techniques.

VARIATIONS

For younger or less competent players, start with more than one fifth columnist per team; require specific kicking or passing methods; when a pass is dropped, the team loses its fifth columnist until players complete 10 accurate passes; use more than one fifth columnist, and if a pass is dropped, the team loses one fifth columnist until a successful pass is made to one of the remaining fifth columnists.

HIT THE CONE

AGES: ALL

Skill execution: 3 ● Decision making: 3 ● Speed: 1

Agility: 2 ● Endurance: 2 ● Speed endurance: 1

OBJECTIVES

To learn how to make correct decisions and accurate passes under pressure.

EQUIPMENT

One ball, six cones

SET-UP

Mark out a 10-by-20-metre to 20-by-30-metre grid with cones, depending on the age and skill level of the players. Place a cone approximately 2 metres from each end, surrounded by a 1-by-1-metre to 2-by-2-metre exclusion zone. Split 8 to 12 players into two equal teams.

HOW TO PLAY

The game starts when you throw the ball into the grid. Each team has a designated cone at one end. Players on the team that catches the ball work to knock their cone over with the ball, but they may not enter the exclusion zone to do so. The players can run with and pass the ball in any direction. Players who are tagged by opponents must stop and pass to a team-mate. If the ball is intercepted, the other team immediately attacks its cone on the other end. If the ball is dropped or passed inaccurately, but not intercepted, the other team gains possession of the ball and you restart play at a sideline. After a team scores (i.e., knocks over the cone), the other team gets the ball, and you restart play behind the end line.

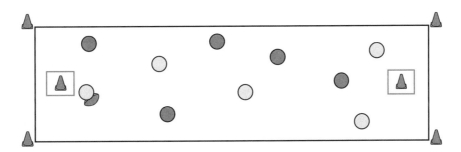

COACHING POINTS

- Players should make accurately weighted passes.
- Players should use good agility and evasion techniques.
- Players should strive for good off-the-ball running and exploitation of space.

VARIATIONS

For younger or less-skilled players, overload the numbers on one of the attacking sides or just play to one end with an overloaded attack; require specific kicking or passing methods; vary the number of times a team can be tagged when in possession (e.g., a team must turn over possession after being tagged three times, or immediately on being tagged once); do not allow players to run with the ball; require older players to do a press-up each time they pass the ball to make the game more physically demanding.

END CORNER BALL

AGES: ALL

Skill execution: 3 ● Decision making: 2 ● Speed: 1

Agility: 2 ● Endurance: 2 ● Speed endurance: 1

OBJECTIVES

To learn how to make correct decisions and accurate passes under pressure.

EQUIPMENT

One ball, four cones

SET-UP

Mark out a 10-by-15-metre to 20-by-30-metre grid with cones, depending on the age and skill level of the players. At each corner, create 1-by-1-metre to 2-by-2-metre exclusion zones. Split 10 to 16 players into two equal teams. Each team is designated an end line, and two players from each team stand inside their corner exclusion zones.

HOW TO PLAY

The game starts when you throw the ball into the grid. Players on the team that catches the ball attempt to get the ball to one of their corner players, but they may not enter the exclusion zone to do so. The players can run with and pass the ball in any direction. Players who are tagged by opponents must stop and pass to a team-mate. If the ball is intercepted, players on the other team immediately attack their end. If the ball is dropped or passed inaccurately, but not intercepted, the other team gains possession of the ball, and you restart play at a sideline. After a team scores (i.e., gets the ball into a corner zone), the other team gets the ball, and you restart play behind the end line.

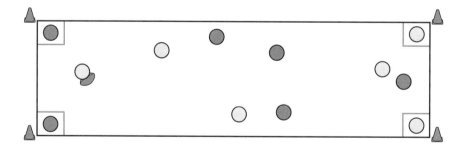

COACHING POINTS

- Players should make accurately weighted passes.
- Players should use good agility and evasion techniques.
- Players should strive for good off-the-ball running and exploitation of space.

VARIATIONS

For younger or less-skilled players, overload the numbers on one of the attacking sides or just play to one end with an overloaded attack; require specific kicking or passing methods; vary the number of times a team can be tagged when in possession (e.g., a team must turn over possession after being tagged three times); do not allow players to run with the ball.

MIXED CORNER BALL

AGES: **ALL**

Skill execution: 2 ● Decision making: 3 ● Speed: 1

Agility: 2 ● Endurance: 2 ● Speed endurance: 1

OBJECTIVES

To learn how to make correct decisions and accurate passes under pressure.

EQUIPMENT

One ball, four cones

SET-UP

Mark out a 10-by-15-metre to 20-by-30-metre grid with cones, depending on the age and skill level of the players. At each corner, create 1-by-1-metre to 2-by-2-metre exclusion zones. Split 12 to 16 players into two equal teams. Two players from each team stand inside a corner exclusion zone, on each end of the grid.

HOW TO PLAY

The game starts when you throw the ball into the grid. Players on the team that catches the ball attempt to get the ball to one of their corner players, but they may not enter the exclusion zone to do so. The players can run with and pass the ball in any direction. Players who are tagged by an opponent must stop and pass to a team-mate. If the ball is intercepted, players on the other team immediately attack and try to get the ball to either of their end players. If the ball is dropped or passed inaccurately, but not intercepted, the other team gains possession of the ball, and you restart play at a sideline. After a team scores (i.e., gets the ball into a corner zone), the corner player immediately passes the ball back into the field to a team-mate, who turns and attacks the other end, attempting to get the ball to the other corner player.

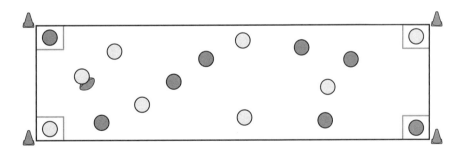

COACHING POINTS

- Players should make accurately weighted passes.
- Players should use good agility and evasion techniques.
- Players should strive for good off-the-ball running and exploitation of space.

VARIATIONS

For younger or less-skilled players, overload the numbers on one of the attacking sides or have only one of the corners at either end occupied; require specific kicking or passing methods; vary the number of times a team can be tagged when in possession (e.g., a team must turn over possession after being tagged one, two, or three times); do not allow players to run with the ball; require older players to do a press-up each time they pass the ball to make the game more physically demanding.

MAT BALL

AGES: ALL

Skill execution: 3 • Decision making: 3 • Speed: 1

Agility: 2 • Endurance: 2 • Speed endurance: 1

OBJECTIVES

To learn how to make correct decisions and accurate passes under pressure.

EQUIPMENT

One ball, four cones, two mats

SET-UP

Mark out a 10-by-15-metre to 20-by-30-metre grid with cones, depending on the age and skill level of the players. Approximately 1 to 2 metres from each end of the grid, place a mat on the ground, surrounded by 2-by-2-metre exclusion zones. Split 10 to 14 players into two equal teams. One player from each team stands on a mat.

HOW TO PLAY

The game starts when you throw the ball for a jump-off in the middle. Players on the team that catches the ball must pass it among themselves (they may not run with the ball) and try to score a point by passing it to the player on the mat. They may not come closer than 2 metres of the mat player. When a team scores (i.e., the ball is passed to the player on the mat), the player on the mat kicks the ball back into play (note, however, that the ball is not alive until it has bounced). If the ball goes out of play, the other team gains possession, and play is restarted at the edge of the grid where it went out.

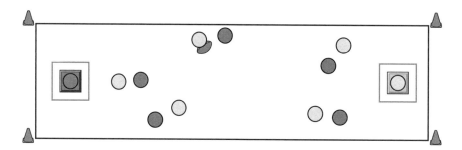

COACHING POINTS

- Players should make accurately weighted passes.
- Players should use good agility and evasion techniques.
- Players should strive for good off-the-ball running and exploitation of space.

VARIATIONS

Allow the players to hold the ball for only three seconds; allow the players to move with the ball and introduce a touch rule (e.g., the opposition can tag the ball carrier, and if the team is touched three times in possession, the other team gets the ball); require that players use a specific type of pass.

RUGBY NETBALL

AGES: ALL

Skill execution: 3 ● Decision making: 3 ● Speed: 1

Agility: 2 ● Endurance: 2 ● Speed endurance: 1

OBJECTIVES

To learn how to make correct decisions and accurate passes under pressure.

EQUIPMENT

One ball, four cones, box or chair

SET-UP

Mark out a 10-by-15-metre to 20-by-30-metre grid with cones, depending on the age and skill level of the players. Split 10 players into two equal teams. One player from each team is outside the grid at each end. The player may be standing or sitting on a box or chair.

HOW TO PLAY

The game starts when you throw the ball into the grid. Players on the team that catches the ball attempt to get the ball to their net (i.e., the player at the end line) to score a goal. The player on the end line may not move. If the ball goes out of play at the side, play restarts with the non-offending team passing the ball in from where it went out of play. The game is restarted by a player on the non-scoring team, who passes the ball back into play from behind the team's end line.

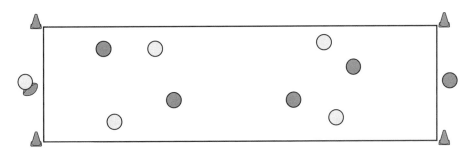

COACHING POINTS

- Players should make accurately weighted passes.
- Players should use good agility and evasion techniques.
- Players should strive for good off-the-ball running and exploitation of space.

VARIATIONS

For younger or less competent players, overload the numbers on one of the attacking sides or have only one "net" and overload the attack; switch the player on the end line after a certain period of time or after each goal; allow the net player to move up and down the end line; place two net players, one from each team, at each end line and allow the net player from the team without the ball to intercept; require specific kicking and passing methods.

CHANNEL BALL

AGES: 12+

Skill execution: 3 ● Decision making: 3 ● Speed: 1

Agility: 3 ● Endurance: 3 ● Speed endurance: 1

OBJECTIVES

To learn how to make correct decisions and accurate passes under pressure and with contact.

EQUIPMENT

One ball, four cones, tackle shields for half the players

SET-UP

Mark out a 10-by-20-metre to 20-by-40-metre grid with cones, depending on the age and skill level of the players. Split 8-14 players into two equal teams, or create an overloaded defence. The ball carriers start at the end of the grid. Players on the other team have tackle shields and stand in a line approximately 5 metres from the ball carriers.

HOW TO PLAY

On your command, players on the team with the ball must make their way through a wall of shields and cross the end line. They must keep the ball alive by hitting and offloading or hitting, spinning, and offloading. If a ball is dropped, all players must sprint back to the start line, and the game begins again. Players who are knocked over must make the ball available in a suitable manner. A player who breaks the line must turn and look for support; the defensive wall must turn and get in an onside position. Once players on the attacking team get to the end of the grid, they immediately turn and attack in the opposite direction. The attackers normally have the ball for a specific period of time (e.g., one minute), and then teams are switched. Count how many times the attackers successfully get to the far end of the grid.

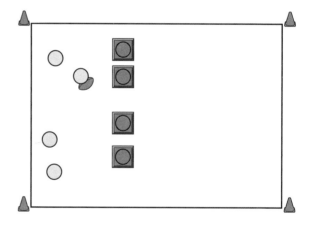

COACHING POINTS

- Support runners must run with commitment.
- Players must make accurate passes in contact, and support runners must time their runs accordingly.

VARIATIONS

Alter the width of the channel and the number of defenders to increase the difficulty for the attacking team to bust the line; allow support players to latch on or to clear the nearest defensive threats; introduce a fullback so that any players breaking the line must have support runners and use them accordingly.

CHAPTER 3

Small-Sided Kicking Games

The small-sided kicking games in this chapter are for a small number of players, usually eight or fewer per team. They exploit the basic techniques of the various kicks found in rugby. Some are suitable as warm-up games for adults, and most can be used as main games for younger and less experienced players. The games are generally of low intensity and would be primarily fun activities for younger children and adults alike.

All players should be able to kick the ball with either foot; they should be competent with basic chip and grubber kicks. Often in a game of rugby, spaces that cannot be exploited by a pass can be exploited by an accurate kick. A well-weighted kick behind the defensive line can cause pressure on the defenders; in rugby league, a kick into the in-goal area can often lead to the attacking side having another set of six tackles. The attacking team can flood through the defensive line and pick up an accurately kicked ball to score a try or regain possession. Accurate kicks over a long distance can relieve the pressure for the kicking team, whereas poorly executed kicks can lead to a rapid counterattack by the opposition.

Kicking, like catching and passing, is a fundamental sport skill and should form part of the basic sport literacy programme of all young rugby players. Because rugby is a late specialisation sport, all players should have adequate kicking skills before they start to concentrate on individual position-specific skills.

The initial games in this chapter (Kick Out, Target Defence, Beat the Guards, Hit the Cone, and Team Skittles) involve kicking towards simple targets; in these games, the kinaesthetic differentiation required to weight a kick is less important. This weighting becomes more important when the games start to require an ability to beat defenders and kick accurately to the far end of the grid. Also note that you can also adapt simple invasion games such as the small-sided handling games in chapter 2 to address kicking. For this reason, only one of these (Rugby Soccer) is described here.

The final games in this chapter are variations of well-known games such as softball and cricket (Rugby Softball, Simple Cricket, and Continuous Cricket). These games further develop aerial catching skills and also introduce longer, accurate kicking from a relatively static position, which players often take up when kicking down field for position. Kicking on the run is a different skill and is developed more in later chapters.

KICK OUT

AGES: ALL

Skill execution: 1 • Decision making: 0 • Speed: 0

Agility: 1 • Endurance: 1 • Speed endurance: 0

OBJECTIVES

To learn how to use the grubber kick and pick up a loose ball.

EQUIPMENT

10 to 20 balls, six cones

SET-UP

Mark out a circle with cones with a radius of 5 to 10 metres, depending on the age and skill level of the players. Inside the circle is a central den that contains 10 to 20 balls. Split up to 20 players into four equal teams. One group of players is inside the circle, and the other groups of players are outside the circle.

HOW TO PLAY

On your command, the players inside the circle attempt to grubber kick the balls outside the circle (they must kick from inside or just outside the den). The players outside the circle pick up the balls and sprint to put them back inside the central den. Count the time it takes the team in the centre to empty the central den of balls. When there are no balls in the central den, teams rotate. The team that expels all its balls in the shortest time is the winner.

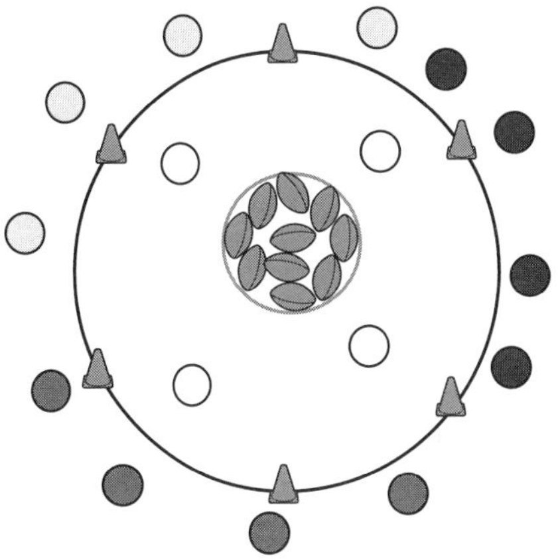

COACHING POINTS

- Players inside the circle should practise accurately kicking into space.
- Players outside the circle should practise accurately stopping or catching the ball.
- Players outside the circle should maintain good agility and speed.

VARIATIONS

For older players, add an outer grid beyond which the kickers are not allowed to kick the ball without receiving a penalty; kickers can be caught out and excluded from the game.

TARGET DEFENCE

AGES: ALL

Skill execution: 2 • Decision making: 0 • Speed: 0

Agility: 1 • Endurance: 1 • Speed endurance: 0

OBJECTIVES

To learn how to use the grubber kick and to catch or pick up a ball.

EQUIPMENT

Up to six balls, 12 cones

SET-UP

Mark out a circle with cones with a radius of 5 to 10 metres depending on the age and skill level of the players. Inside the circle is a central den that contains up to six cones spaced far enough apart that they won't knock each other over if they fall. Split 8 to 16 players into two equal teams. One group of players is inside the circle; the other group of players is outside. Some of the players outside the circle have balls.

HOW TO PLAY

On your command, the players outside the circle attempt to grubber kick their balls into the circle to knock over the cones. The players inside the circle catch or pick up the balls and roll them back outside the circle. Record the number of cones the outside players knock over in a specific time period; then have the teams rotate. The team that scores highest is the winner.

COACHING POINTS

- Players outside the circle should use good kicking skills.
- Players inside the circle should use good catching technique.
- Players should maintain good agility and speed.

VARIATIONS

The players outside the circle can pick up balls and pass them to players who are in more advantageous positions to kick; the players inside the circle pick up balls and sprint with them to the outside of the circle; the players inside the circle pick up balls and grubber kick them to the outside of the circle; players inside the circle are penalised if they drop or knock a ball forward with their hands or arms so that it touches the ground.

BEAT THE GUARDS

AGES: ALL

Skill execution: 2 ● Decision making: 0 ● Speed: 0

Agility: 1 ● Endurance: 0 ● Speed endurance: 0

OBJECTIVES
To learn how to use the grubber kick and catch or pick up a ball.

EQUIPMENT
One ball, four cones

SET-UP
Mark out a 10-by-20-metre grid with cones, and create a 1- to 2-metre channel in the centre. Split up to 12 players into two equal teams. One team stands inside the centre channel, and the other team splits in two and goes to either end of the grid.

HOW TO PLAY
The ball starts with a player at one end of the grid who grubber kicks it through the team in the centre channel to team-mates at the far end of the grid. Teams gain a point for each kick successfully collected by a player at the other end. If a player at the far end fumbles the ball while catching or picking it up, no point is scored. Players in the centre channel try to stop the ball and roll it back to the outside team. The game is played for a specific period of time, and the teams then switch. The team that ends with the most points wins.

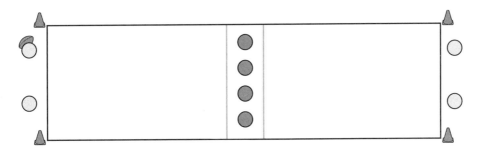

COACHING POINTS
- Players should practise kicking accurately into space.
- Players should carefully collect rolling balls.

VARIATIONS
Use more than one ball; allow the players to pass the ball to team-mates who are in more advantageous positions; players in the centre channel who stop the ball take it to the sideline, and the end players have to sprint round to collect it.

HIT THE CONE

AGES: ALL

Skill execution: 2 ● Decision making: 0 ● Speed: 0

Agility: 2 ● Endurance: 0 ● Speed endurance: 0

OBJECTIVES

To develop basic kicking skills, particularly the grubber kick, and to develop basic catching skills.

EQUIPMENT

One ball, 10 to 20 cones

SET-UP

Mark out a 5-by-10-metre to 10-by-20-metre grid, depending on the age and skill level of the players, with cones at each end of the grid, spaced approximately 1 metre apart. A centre line is marked on the grid. Split 6 to 12 players into two equal teams. Each team stands on one half of the grid.

HOW TO PLAY

A player from one team grubber kicks the ball into the opponents' half of the grid in an attempt to knock down the opponents' cones. Players from the other team try to catch the bouncing ball or stop it with their feet. Players who catch or stop the ball must kick it back over and attempt to knock down the cones at the other end. The team that knocks down all of the opponents' cones first is the winner.

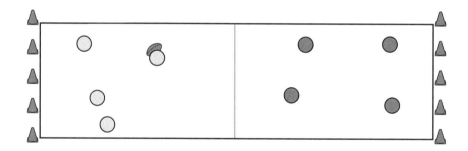

COACHING POINTS

- Players should practise accurately weighted kicks.
- Players should use good individual and team communication when catching the ball.

VARIATIONS

Introduce more balls; allow the player who stops or catches the ball to pass to a team-mate who is in a better position to kick the ball; penalise any players who, while stopping a kick, drop or knock the ball forward with their hands or arms so that it touches the ground (e.g., make them pass the ball back to the other team and forego their team's kick).

TEAM SKITTLES

AGES: ALL

Skill execution: 2 ● Decision making: 1 ● Speed: 0

Agility: 2 ● Endurance: 1 ● Speed endurance: 0

OBJECTIVES

To learn how to use grubber kicks and make accurate passes under pressure.

EQUIPMENT

One ball, 14 to 16 cones (skittles)

SET-UP

Mark out a 10-by-15-metre to 20-by- 30-metre grid, depending on the age and skill level of the players, with a group of 5 or 6 cones (skittles) at each end of the grid. The cones are inside a 1- to 2-metre exclusion zone, which should be approximately 1 metre from the end line. A centre line is marked on the grid. Split 10 players into two equal teams.

HOW TO PLAY

The game starts when you throw the ball into the grid. Each team has a designated end. The team that catches the ball then attempts to get the ball to the opponents' end and to knock over the opponents' skittles. Ball carriers may not move but may pass the ball in any direction and must stay within their half of the court. If the other team catches the ball, it attacks the skittles at the other end. After a point is scored (i.e., the team with the ball knocks over an opponent's skittle), the other team gains possession of the ball and restarts play behind its end line. The team that knocks down all of the opponents' skittles first is the winner.

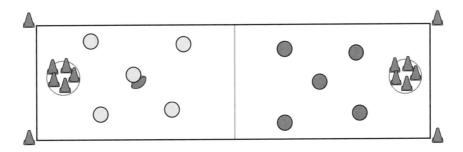

COACHING POINTS

- Players should strive to make accurate passes and kicks.
- Players should use good individual and team communication.

VARIATIONS

Require specific kicking and passing methods (e.g., players may only kick to each other, or players must have had the ball passed to them before they can attempt to knock down a cone); use more than one ball.

RUGBY SOCCER

AGES: 12+

Skill execution: 2 • Decision making: 2 • Speed: 4

Agility: 2 • Endurance: 3 • Speed endurance: 1

OBJECTIVES
To develop basic kicking and passing skills.

EQUIPMENT
One soccer ball, four cones

SET-UP
Mark out a 30-by-40-metre grid with a soccer goal set up at each end. Divide the grid into four zones. Split 10-16 players into two equal teams. One player from each team acts as a goalkeeper; all other players position within the grid.

HOW TO PLAY
The game is started with a soccer-style kick from the centre of the field. Players on the team in possession can pass along the ground to other players' feet. A ball kicked into the air can be caught by players from either team with their hands. A player who catches the ball can run with it for 5 metres before kicking it. If the ball bounces when it is kicked to another player, it cannot be caught but must be played with the feet. A player who catches a ball before it has bounced can kick it from the hands or soccer-style kick it from the ground. To score, players must kick the ball through the goal. They cannot score from outside the zone nearest the opponents' goal.

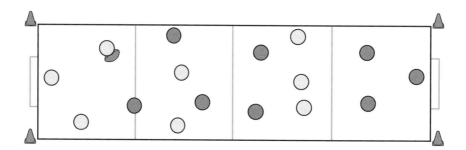

COACHING POINTS
- Players should strive for accurate kicks.
- Players in possession of the ball should use good communication.
- The team in possession of the ball should use good catching techniques.

VARIATIONS
The team in possession must bounce the ball while running; the goalkeeper changes after every goal or period of time; teams play without goalkeepers, and any player can attempt to save a shot on goal.

RUGBY SOFTBALL

AGES: ALL

Skill execution: 2 ● Decision making: 1 ● Speed: 2

Agility: 2 ● Endurance: 1 ● Speed endurance: 0

OBJECTIVES

To develop basic kicking and passing skills.

EQUIPMENT

One ball, four cones

SET-UP

Mark out a diamond-shaped 10-by-10-metre to 20-by-20-metre grid, depending on the age and skill level of the players. Place cones at each corner of the diamond and mark "baselines" between the cones. Split up to 16 players into two equal teams. The batting team lines up behind one of the cones (home plate). The fielding team positions deep, behind the imaginary line that runs through first and third base.

HOW TO PLAY

The first player in the batting line kicks the ball and runs. The ball must be land either in the outfield or in the infield beyond first and third base. A player is out if the kicked ball is caught before it has bounced. One point is scored each time a player crosses home plate. A run is not counted if the player leaves the base before the ball is kicked or if a player is out during that kick. A player occupying a base is out if another runner arrives at the base. A runner is out if tagged with the ball before reaching a base, the fielder with the ball gets to the base before the runner, or the runner runs more than 1 metre out of the baseline to avoid being tagged. Fielders can kick the ball in from the outfield, but they must use a pass to tag a runner out. The pass must hit the runner between the waist and shoulders.

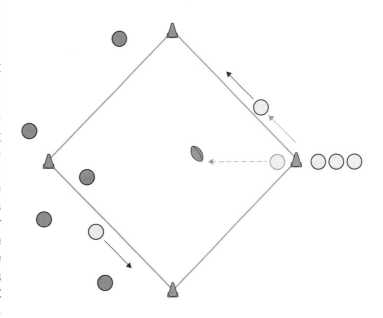

COACHING POINTS

- Players should practise accurate kicks.
- Players on the fielding team should use good communication.
- Players on the fielding team should use good catching techniques.

VARIATION

A fielder can tag a runner with the ball for an out.

SIMPLE CRICKET

AGES: ALL

Skill execution: 2 ● Decision making: 1 ● Speed: 2

Agility: 2 ● Endurance: 1 ● Speed endurance: 0

OBJECTIVE

To develop basic kicking skills.

EQUIPMENT

One ball, six cones

SET-UP

Mark out a 10-by-15-metre to 20-by-30-metre grid with cones, depending on the age and skill level of the players, and place a cone approximately 1 metre from each end line to represent a wicket. Split 10 to 16 players into two equal teams. One batter stands with a ball behind a wicket at one end and the rest of the team lines up behind the end line. Two players from the fielding team position next to the wickets at each end, and the remaining players position throughout the grid.

HOW TO PLAY

The first batter kicks the ball into the field and runs. The batter's partner is at the other wicket. The ball must bounce in the field of play, or the player is out. A player scores a run by running to the far wicket. A player may choose to stay at the far wicket, but only if another team-mate is not already there. A run is disallowed if a player leaves the wicket before the ball is kicked or if the player at bat is out during that kick. A player is out if the kicked ball is caught before it has bounced, a fielder with the ball gets to the wicket before the runner, or a fielder passes to the player at the wicket before the runner gets there. When the ball is finally in the possession of a wicket player, it is then returned to the batter at the starting wicket, who can kick it again. The batting team scores four points if the ball is kicked out with a bounce through the far end, at which point the batter gets another attempt. Teams switch after all players in line have had a turn.

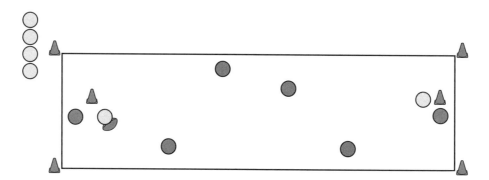

COACHING POINTS

- Players on the batting team should practise accurate kicking.
- Players on the fielding team should use good catching and passing techniques.
- Players on the fielding team should use good communication.

VARIATIONS

Have only one batter at a time and if the batter gets to the far wicket, he can elect to walk back to the near wicket to take the kick; give the batting team two points for kicking the ball out of the sidelines; allow the fielding team to kick the ball back to the wickets; the batting team starts with 50 points, each batter has a specific number of kicks, and rather than being out, batting teams lose a certain number of points.

CONTINUOUS CRICKET

AGES: ALL

Skill execution: 2 ● Decision making: 1 ● Speed: 2

Agility: 2 ● Endurance: 2 ● Speed endurance: 1

OBJECTIVES

To learn how to use the grubber kick and to pick up a loose ball.

EQUIPMENT

One ball, one mat, seven cones

SET-UP

Mark out a 30-by-30-metre to 50-by-50-metre grid with cones, depending on the age and skill level of the players. Place a mat and cone at the centre of one end line, approximately 1 metre in from the end line; parallel to the cone and mat (you can also use a tackle shield), place another cone approximately 5 metres away (this should be at the leg side for a right-handed batsman). Place another cone approximately 10 metres into the grid, directly opposite the mat. Split up to 20 players into two equal teams. The batting team lines up outside the grid, behind the end line. The fielding team positions inside the grid with one player acting as the bowler (with less skilled players, you can be the bowler) and another as wicket keeper.

HOW TO PLAY

The first player in the batting line stands in front of the mat. The bowler passes or rolls the ball, and the batter must kick or catch and kick the ball forward (i.e., no back-hits allowed). Whether the ball is kicked or not, the batter must run to the far wicket (cone) and back to the starting wicket (cone) to score a point. A batter is out if the kicked ball is caught before it has bounced or if the bowler hits the stumps (mat) with the ball. The batting team scores four points if the ball is kicked out with a bounce beyond the far end line; the batting team scores six points if the ball goes beyond the boundary without a bounce. The fielders can pass or kick the ball back to the bowler by using passes and kicks between them. The bowler can bowl (i.e., pass or roll) as soon as the ball arrives irrespective of whether the batter is back in front of the stumps. As soon as a batter is out, the next batter in line takes a turn (the new batter must step up quickly or risk being bowled out before arriving!). Switch teams after all batters in line have had a turn.

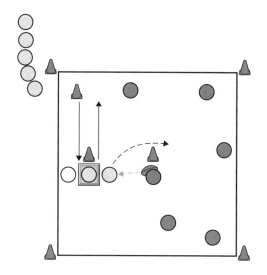

COACHING POINTS

- Batters should practise kicking accurately into space.
- Players on the fielding team should use good kicks, passes, and catches.
- Players on the fielding team should use good communication.

VARIATION

The bowler can use a grubber kick.

Attacking and Defensive Drills

Attacking and defensive drills are for a small number of players, usually eight or fewer per activity or at one given time. They are designed to improve basic attack and defensive techniques and decision making in various situations by creating gamelike scenarios.

When a team is in possession, rugby is about creating space and exploiting situations in which there is a discrepancy in numbers in favour of the attacking team. Attacking players should be able to exploit a 3v2 or 2v1 situation by fixing defenders and accurately passing the ball to a team-mate in space. Defenders must be able to identify such situations and react accordingly, constantly adjusting in an effort to nullify the attacking threat.

In drills such as those found in this chapter, ball carriers can learn various methods of creating space such as fixing defenders and committing them away from the space to be exploited by a support runner, or attracting defenders and moving them to create space for the support runners. The support runners will learn the importance of running good lines to exploit the spaces created by the ball carrier, as well as how to create their own space for the ball carrier by adjusting their lines of run late to get away from defending players. The defending players learn the key points of situational defence against various lines of attack.

Most of these drills form the 'part' of the whole-part-whole concept by breaking down the bigger attacking or defensive picture into smaller parts to analyse the individual components. These drills should not just be used in isolation because players can become very comfortable with and successful at exploiting 3v2 situations within a channel with defined boundaries and numbers, but then be unable to transfer this into the wider context of the game.

Most of these drills can also be used as conditioning activities by altering the space, timing, and number of players. However, before you do so, make sure the players are competent in the drill and are adept at using their core skills and making good decisions within the context of the drill when in a non-fatigued state. If the drill is continually breaking down because of poor execution, the conditioning element will not be sufficient. On the other hand, if players can perform the drill perfectly under extreme fatigue, it is likely not challenging enough. Most of the drills are presented as 2v1 and 3v2 situations, but these could be enhanced into 4v3 situations if skill and decision-making ability allows. Conversely, with younger or less skilled players, the situations could even be presented as 3v1.

Although the activities are presented as drills because they are in a defined space and present the players with specific scenarios, with the addition of a timed event and point scoring, you can introduce a game element. In addition, many can be combined with interval shuttles or combined with bag or shield drills (which you will learn more about in chapter 5) to exhaust players so you can test their skills or mental concentration when fatigued.

HIT AND SPIN RELAY

AGES: ALL

Skill execution: 1   ● Decision making: 0   ● Speed: 1

Agility: 2   ● Endurance: 2   ● Speed endurance: 0

OBJECTIVES

To learn how to use footwork, turn prior to or on contact, and make the ball available.

EQUIPMENT

One ball, two tackle shields, four cones

SET-UP

Mark out a 5-by-10-metre grid. Split up to 16 players into two equal groups. One player from each group stands in the centre of the grid, holding a tackle shield. The rest of the players in each group line up behind an end line, opposite this player. The first player in one line has a ball.

HOW TO PLAY

On your command, the player with the ball runs towards the centre player and hits and spins and then continues to sprint forward before passing backwards to the oncoming player from the opposite group. The drill continues until all players in both lines have had a turn.

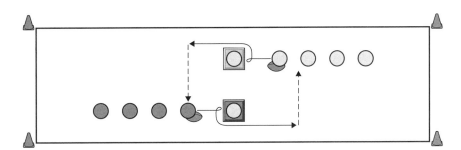

COACHING POINTS

- Ball carriers should use good footwork prior to passing.
- Opposite runners should be able to time their runs to make the catch.
- Ball carriers should maintain possession during contact.

VARIATION

Players at the front of each line start with a ball and pass to the second player in the next line.

HIT AND SPIN

AGES: 12+

Skill execution: 2 • Decision making: 0 • Speed: 1

Agility: 2 • Endurance: 1 • Speed endurance: 1

OBJECTIVES

To learn how to use footwork, turn prior to or on contact, and make the ball available; for support runners, to learn how to vary their depth and attack the space effectively.

EQUIPMENT

One ball, three tackle shields, four cones

SET-UP

Mark out a 15-by-15-metre grid with cones. Split seven players into groups of four attackers and three defenders. The four attackers line up at the end of the grid; the player nearest the sideline is in possession of the ball. The three defenders hold shields and line up across the centre of the grid.

HOW TO PLAY

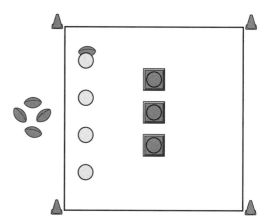

On your command, the attackers move forward with the ball; the first ball carrier must hit, spin, and pass the ball to another player, who must do likewise until the ball is released to the free player, who can score unopposed. The runners may not score by busting the pads using leg drives and upper-body contact to break through a small gap between adjacent defenders. The defenders may only move sideways. When the players get to the other side of the grid, they turn and attack the opposite end of the grid. If the attackers lose possession, they turn and collect another ball.

COACHING POINTS

- Ball carriers should use good footwork prior to reaching the defenders.
- Support runners should have the ability to properly time their runs.
- Ball carriers should strive to maintain possession during contact.

VARIATIONS

Make the grid longer and introduce a fullback to encourage support play, and have everyone try to get through the line; the defenders can advance rather than just move side to side.

2V1V1 DRILL

AGES: 11+

Skill execution: 2 ● Decision making: 1 ● Speed: 1

Agility: 2 ● Endurance: 2 ● Speed endurance: 2

OBJECTIVES

To develop the ability to fix a defender, make quick decisions, and make accurate short passes while fatigued; to learn how to work off the ball, identify space, and time the support run.

EQUIPMENT

One ball, four cones

SET-UP

Mark out a 5-by-5-metre to 15-by-15-metre grid with cones, depending on the age and skill level of the players. Split players into groups of four (two attackers and two defenders). The two attackers start in the middle of the grid, and the defenders start at each end of the grid.

HOW TO PLAY

Pass the ball to one of the attackers. On receiving the ball, the two attackers attack one defender. The attacker with the ball attempts to fix the defender and pass to the other attacker, who is in space. When the attackers cross the end line, they score a point and immediately turn and attack in the other direction. The other defender may not leave the line to defend until both attackers have turned to attack him. If the attackers drop the ball, feed another ball, at which point they should immediately turn and attack in the other direction. If they keep possession but fail to score, the same applies. Attackers and defenders switch after a specific period of time, normally between 30 and 60 seconds.

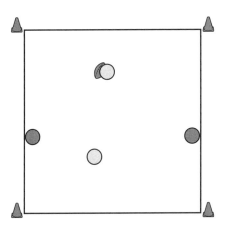

COACHING POINTS

- Ball carriers need to fix and draw opponents towards them and away from support runners.
- Support runners must hold their width and time their runs correctly.
- Attacking players must communicate with each other.

VARIATIONS

The defenders hold shields to allow for contact; set up groups of three in which the defender retreats to the try line at the far end of the grid after each attack, and the attackers continue attacking.

2V1+1 DRILL

AGES: 12+

Skill execution: 2 • Decision making: 2 • Speed: 2

Agility: 2 • Endurance: 2 • Speed endurance: 2

OBJECTIVES

To develop the ability to fix a defender, make quick decisions, and make short, accurate passes while fatigued; to learn how to work off the ball, identify space, and time support runs.

EQUIPMENT

One ball, four cones

SET-UP

Mark out a 10-by-10-metre to 15-by-15-metre grid with cones, depending on the age and skill level of the players. Split players into groups of four (two attackers and two defenders). The two attackers start along one end of the grid, and the defenders start in the middle of the grid, lined up behind each other, approximately 5 metres apart.

HOW TO PLAY

Pass the ball to one of the attackers. On receiving the ball, both attackers attack the first defender. The attacker with the ball attempts to fix the first defender and then passes to the other attacker, who is in space. When the attackers have beaten the first defender, they immediately move on to attack the second defender. The second defender may not move forward to defend until both attackers have beaten the first defender. If the attackers successfully beat both defenders and reach the other end, they immediately turn around and attack the other way, the defenders also having turned around. If the attackers drop the ball, they immediately return to their starting positions, and you restart play by feeding another ball. If they keep possession but fail to score, the same applies. Attackers and defenders switch after a specific period of time, normally between 30 and 60 seconds.

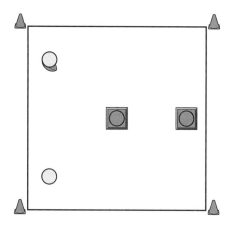

COACHING POINTS

- Ball carriers should fix and draw opponents towards them and away from support runners.
- Support runners must hold their width and time their runs correctly.
- Attacking players must communicate with each other.

VARIATIONS

The defenders hold shields, allowing for contact; set up groups of four in which the defenders retreat to the try line at the far end of the grid after each attack before turning to defend one after the other, and the attackers then continue attacking.

CONTINUAL 3V2+2

AGES: 12+

Skill execution: 3 ● Decision making: 3 ● Speed: 2

Agility: 2 ● Endurance: 3 ● Speed endurance: 2

OBJECTIVES

To develop the ability to fix or drag a defender, make quick decisions, and make short, accurate passes while fatigued; to learn how to work off the ball, identify space, and run correct lines; to learn how to mentally switch from defence to offence.

EQUIPMENT

One ball, four cones

SET-UP

Mark out a 15-by-15-metre grid with cones. Split players into groups of seven (three attackers and four defenders). The three attackers start in the middle of the grid, and two defenders are at each end of the grid.

HOW TO PLAY

Pass the ball to one of the attackers (A1). On receiving the ball, the attackers attack the first group of two defenders (D1 and D2). When the attackers score, the two original defenders become attackers; the ball carrier and these two defenders immediately turn and attack in the other direction while the other two attackers (A2 and A3) stay and become defenders. The third and fourth defenders (D3 and D4), who are positioned at the other end of the grid, may not leave their line to defend until the ball carrier and D1 and D2 (who are now attackers) have turned to attack them. When the attackers score, the two defenders (D3 and D4) become attackers; the ball carrier and these two defenders immediately turn and attack in the other direction while the other two attackers (D1 and D2) stay and defend. If the attackers drop the ball or fail to score, players immediately turn and attack in the other direction. The drill continues for a specified period of time, normally between one and three minutes.

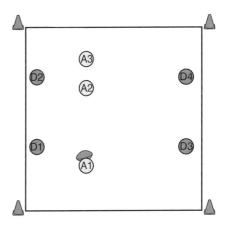

COACHING POINTS

- Ball carriers need to fix and draw their opponents towards them and away from the support runners, or drag an opponent out of position to create space on the inside of the defender.
- Support runners must hold their width and time their runs correctly.
- Attacking players must communicate with each other.

VARIATIONS

The defenders hold shields, allowing for contact; use five players (three attackers and two defenders) and have the defenders retreat to the try line at the far end of the grid after each attack, at which point the attackers continue attacking.

BREAKOUT

AGES: 14+

Skill execution: 3 • Decision making: 3 • Speed: 2

Agility: 2 • Endurance: 2 • Speed endurance: 1

OBJECTIVES

To develop the ability to attack from different directions, identify space, and hold defenders; to develop defensive communication.

EQUIPMENT

One ball, eight cones

SET-UP

Mark out a small 8-by-10-metre grid with cones. This grid is surrounded by a larger 12-by-15-metre grid, depending on the age and skill level of your players. Place a cone at each corner of each grid. Split players into groups of seven or eight (three or four attackers and four defenders). The attacking players position inside the smaller middle grid, and one player has a ball. The defenders each position along a sideline in the larger outside grid.

HOW TO PLAY

On your command, the attackers attack a defender at one of the sidelines, creating a 3v1 situation, and attempt to score by getting the ball over the outside lines. The other defenders may move around the outside channel to assist a defender under pressure. If the attackers score, they must re-enter the central square and initiate another attack. Attacking players who are touched while in possession must immediately pass to another player, who will attack another axis. All passes must be lateral or backwards relative to the direction that in which the player is running. After receiving a pass, a player may choose to attack another axis if a better opportunity presents itself. The attackers have a set number of touches or time in possession in which to score as many tries as possible after which the attackers and defenders switch roles.

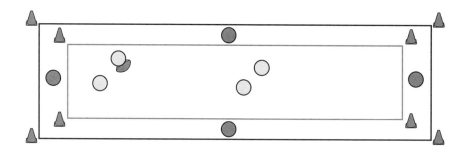

COACHING POINTS

- Ball carriers need to fix and draw their opponents towards them and away from the support runners, or drag opponents out of position to create space on the inside of the defender.
- Support runners must be alert to attacking opportunities around the whole grid and communicate accordingly.

3V2 TWO-MINUTE DRILL

AGES: 14+

Skill execution: 3 • Decision making: 3 • Speed: 1

Agility: 2 • Endurance: 4 • Speed endurance: 3

OBJECTIVES

To develop the ability to fix a defender, make quick decisions, and make short, accurate passes while fatigued; to learn how to work off the ball, identify space, and time the support run.

EQUIPMENT

Four balls, four cones

SET-UP

Mark out a 10-by-20-metre to 10-by-30-metre grid with cones, depending on the age and skill level of your players. Split players into groups of five (three attackers and two defenders). All players line up along one end line, alternating between attackers and defenders. The attackers are lying on their chests, and the defenders are standing. One attacker has a ball.

HOW TO PLAY

On your command, the attackers get to their feet and the defenders sprint 10 metres to the opposite end line before turning and defending. The attackers attempt to fix the defenders and attack space. When touched, attacking players go back onto their chests, regain their feet, and tap the ball; the defenders retreat a required distance (3, 5, 7, or 10 metres). Attackers who drop the ball immediately turn around and collect a ball from behind the end line. If the attackers cross the goal line with the ball, play restarts at the far end of the grid. Switch after two minutes.

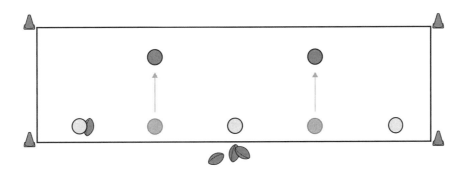

COACHING POINTS

- Ball carriers need to fix and draw their opponents towards them and away from the support runners, or drag them out of position thereby creating space on the inside of the defender.
- Support runners must hold their width and time runs correctly.
- Attacking players must communicate with each other.

VARIATION

Perform the drill in a smaller grid (5 to 10 metres long) for only one tackle, after which this is immediately repeated from the other end.

4V2V2 DRILL

AGES: 14+

Skill execution: 3 • Decision making: 3 • Speed: 2

Agility: 2 • Endurance: 4 • Speed endurance: 2

OBJECTIVES

To develop the ability to fix or drag a defender, make quick decisions, and make short, accurate passes while fatigued; to learn how to work off the ball, identify space, and run the correct lines.

EQUIPMENT

One ball, four cones

SET-UP

Mark out a 10-by-15-metre to 20-by-20-metre grid with cones, depending on the age and skill level of your players. Split players into groups of eight (four attackers and four defenders). The four attackers start in the middle of the grid, and two defenders start at each end of the grid.

HOW TO PLAY

Pass the ball to one of the attackers (A1). On receiving the ball, the attackers attack two defenders at one end of the grid (D1 and D2). When the attackers score, they immediately turn in the other direction and attack the two defenders at the other end (D3 and D4). These two defenders may not leave their line to defend until the attackers have turned to attack them. If the attackers drop the ball, they immediately turn and attack in the other direction using a ball you have fed to them. If they keep possession but fail to score, the same applies. Attackers and defenders switch positions after a specific period of time, normally between 30 and 60 seconds.

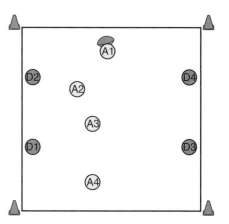

COACHING POINTS

- Ball carriers need to fix and draw their opponents towards them and away from the support runners, or drag opponents out of position thereby creating space on the inside of the defender.
- Support runners must hold their width and time their runs correctly.
- Attacking players must communicate with each other.

VARIATION

The defenders hold shields, allowing for contact.

4V2+2 DRILL

AGES: 14+

Skill execution: 4 ● Decision making: 3 ● Speed: 2

Agility: 2 ● Endurance: 4 ● Speed endurance: 2

OBJECTIVES

To develop the ability to fix or drag a defender, make quick decisions, and make short, accurate passes while fatigued; to learn how to work off the ball, identify space, and run the correct lines.

EQUIPMENT

Five balls, four cones

SET-UP

Mark out a 10-by-15-metre to 20-by-20-metre grid with cones, depending on the age and skill level of your players. Split players into groups of eight (four attackers and four defenders). The four attackers start along one end line, two defenders start approximately one third of the way into the grid, and the other two defenders start approximately two thirds into the grid.

HOW TO PLAY

On your command, the attackers attack the first two defenders (D1 and D2). When the attackers beat these defenders, they immediately attack the next two defenders (D3 and D4). Defenders D3 and D4 may not leave their line to defend until D1 and D2 have been beaten. If the attackers score, they immediately turn and attack in the other direction, this time attacking D3 and D4 first. If the attackers drop the ball, they immediately turn and collect a ball from behind the line. If they keep possession but fail to score, the same applies. Attackers and defenders switch positions after a specific period of time, normally between 30 and 60 seconds.

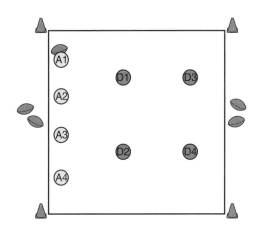

COACHING POINTS

- Ball carriers need to fix and draw their opponents towards them and away from the support runners, or drag opponents out of position thereby creating space on the inside of the defender.
- Support runners must hold their width and time their runs correctly.
- Attacking players must communicate with each other.

VARIATIONS

Defenders may only move laterally; defenders hold shields, allowing for contact.

3V5 ONE-TACKLE DEFENCE

AGES: 12+

Skill execution: 3 • Decision making: 3 • Speed: 2

Agility: 3 • Endurance: 2 • Speed endurance: 1

OBJECTIVES

For attackers and defenders to practise communication skills and decision making.

EQUIPMENT

Five balls, four cones

SET-UP

Mark out a 15-by-15-metre to 20-by-20-metre grid with cones, depending on the age and skill level of your players. Split players into groups of eight, and label them 1 through 8. Players start by lying in the middle of the grid, either on their chests or backs. Place five balls along one end line.

HOW TO PLAY

To begin play, call out three player numbers; these players become the defenders. On hearing the call, the three defenders run to the end line behind them, turn, and prepare to defend. Each player whose number was not called runs to the other end, one player picks up a ball, and the players attack. The attackers attempt to score with accurate passes and by running good option lines as decoys or supporting the ball carrier. When a player in possession is touched or crosses the end line, play restarts.

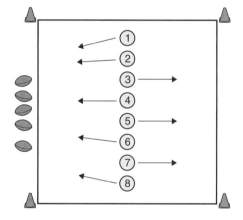

COACHING POINTS

- Defenders mark the inside or outside shoulder of the attackers in front of them and then drift, or wedge, onto the next player depending on the situation.
- Defenders need to keep their hips facing forward and not allow attacking players to beat them on their inside shoulders.
- Defenders must communicate clearly with each other.

VARIATIONS

Require that defenders go around a specific cone or cones; alter the numbers of attackers and defenders.

SOUTH-WEST-NORTH-EAST

AGES: 14+

Skill execution: 2 • Decision making: 2 • Speed: 1

Agility: 1 • Endurance: 2 • Speed endurance: 1

OBJECTIVES

For defenders to practise communication skills and decision making.

EQUIPMENT

One ball, four cones

SET-UP

Mark out a 15-by-15-metre to 20-by-20-metre grid with cones, depending on the age and skill level of your players. Split players into groups of seven. Four attackers position along the south end of the grid, and a corner player has the ball. Three defenders position inside the grid, anywhere from 3 to 10 metres back, facing the attackers.

HOW TO PLAY

The attackers begin the activity by passing the ball to each other from the corner of the grid. As the first ball carrier passes the ball, the defender moves from that player to the next. When a tackle is made, or if the attackers score, the attackers move clockwise and realign along the west side of the grid, and the defenders realign accordingly.

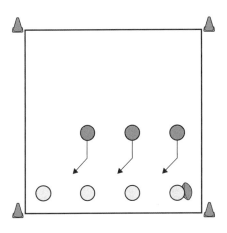

COACHING POINTS

- Defenders should mark the inside shoulder of the attacker in front of them and then drift onto the next player.
- Defenders need to keep their hips facing forward and not allow attacking players to beat them on their inside shoulders.
- Defenders must communicate clearly with each other.

VARIATION

Add a second group of attackers on the west side of the grid and have them start with the ball on the opposite corner, causing the defenders to wedge in from the outside shoulder of the attackers.

3V4 DEFENCE GRID

AGES: 14+

Skill execution: 3 • Decision making: 3 • Speed: 1

Agility: 2 • Endurance: 2 • Speed endurance: 1

OBJECTIVES
For defenders to practise communication skills and decision making.

EQUIPMENT
Four balls, four cones

SET-UP
Mark out a 15-by-15-metre to 20-by-20-metre grid with cones, depending on the age and skill level of your players. Split players into groups of 19 (four groups of four attackers and one group of three defenders). Position four attackers along each side of the grid, and give a ball to an end player on each side. The defenders position inside the grid facing one group of attackers.

HOW TO PLAY
One group of attackers begins the activity by passing the ball to each other. The defenders move forward and nominate an attacker to tackle. When a tackle is made, or if the attackers score (i.e., get to the opposite side of the grid without being tackled), the defenders go back to the centre of the grid and face another group of attackers. Play continues until all attackers have gone, or for a specified period of time.

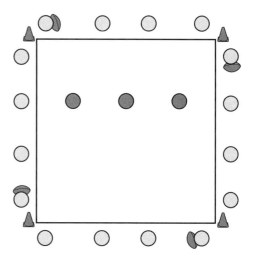

COACHING POINTS
- Defenders should mark the inside or outside shoulder of the attacker in front of them and then drift, or wedge, onto the next player depending on the situation.
- Defenders need to keep their hips facing forward and not allow attacking players to beat them on their inside shoulders.
- Defenders must communicate clearly with each other.

VARIATIONS
With reduced numbers, use less than four groups or by using 3 v 2 situations; require the defenders to start on their chests or backs before each group of players attacks; speed the activity up so that the defenders do not have a chance to realign before the next wave of attackers come through.

2V3 GATE DEFENCE

AGES: 12+

Skill execution: 3 ● Decision making: 2 ● Speed: 2

Agility: 2 ● Endurance: 2 ● Speed endurance: 2

OBJECTIVES

For attackers and defenders to practise communication skills and decision making.

EQUIPMENT

Five balls, four cones

SET-UP

Mark out a 15-by-15-metre to 20-by-20-metre grid with cones, depending on the age and skill level of your players. Split players into groups of five and position them behind one sideline, in the centre. The players are numbered 1 to 5. Place five balls behind one end line

HOW TO PLAY

The activity starts when you call two numbers. The players with those numbers are the defenders. On hearing the call, the two defenders run to the side opposite the side with the balls, turn, and prepare to defend. The players whose numbers were not called run to the other side, one player picks up a ball, and the group attacks. The attacking players attempt to beat the two defenders using good footwork and ball techniques. The defenders move forward and attempt to tackle the player with the ball. When the ball is passed from one attacker to another, the defenders slide onto the new ball carrier. At the end of each attack, the players go back to their starting positions and prepare for new numbers to be called. The drill typically lasts for two to three minutes.

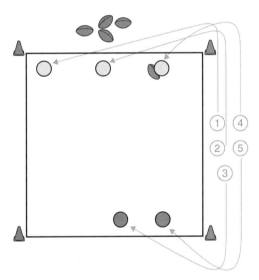

COACHING POINTS

- Defenders should mark the inside or outside shoulder of the attacker in front of them and then drift, or wedge, onto the next player depending on the situation.
- Defenders need to keep their hips facing forward and not allow attacking players to beat them on their inside shoulders.
- Defenders must communicate clearly with each other.

VARIATIONS

Require players to start on their chests or backs; require the defenders to go around a specific cone or cones; alter the numbers of attackers and defenders.

COVER ADJUSTMENT DRILL

AGES: 14+

Skill execution: 3 ● Decision making: 2 ● Speed: 2

Agility: 2 ● Endurance: 1 ● Speed endurance: 1

OBJECTIVES

For attackers and defenders to practise communication skills and decision making, particularly those who defend in the outside channels such as centres and wingers.

EQUIPMENT

One ball, four cones

SET-UP

Mark out a 15-by-15-metre to 20-by-20-metre grid with cones, depending on the age and skill level of your players. Split players into groups of four. One attacker and defender are in the grid. The attacker has a ball. The other two players stand along the sideline, and each is given a number.

HOW TO PLAY

The activity starts when you call a number to nominate which outside player will become a second attacker. The player whose number was not called then becomes a second defender. These players enter the grid. On hearing the call, the two attackers try to score against the two defenders. Play restarts after each attack. Play typically lasts for one to two minutes.

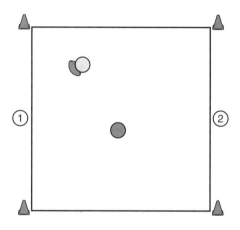

COACHING POINTS

- The initial defender must not get drawn into a 2v1 situation but must work with the new defender to gain time to create a 2v2 situation.
- The two defenders must communicate clearly to stop the attackers from scoring.

COVER AND CHASE

AGES: 14+

Skill execution: 3 ● Decision making: 2 ● Speed: 3

Agility: 2 ● Endurance: 1 ● Speed endurance: 3

OBJECTIVE

For attackers and defenders to practise communication skills and decision making, particularly when covering back to defend against a line break.

EQUIPMENT

One ball, eight cones

SET-UP

Mark out a 15-by-20-metre to 20-by-20-metre grid with cones, depending on the age and skill level of your players. Place cones inside the grid, as indicated in the diagram (these locations are a guide and can be adjusted to suit the ability of your players). Split up to 16 players into four equal groups. Players position at the cones as shown.

HOW TO PLAY

On your command, the two attackers (attacking ball carrier [A1] and attacking winger [A2]) try to score, and the covering defender (D1) and fullback (D2) communicate and try to stop the attackers from scoring. The attackers have only one tackle in which to score by placing the ball over the goal line. When the attack is complete, the players go to the end of their respective lines. The activity typically lasts for three minutes.

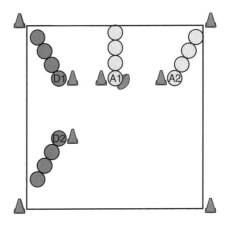

COACHING POINTS

- Defenders must work together to put the attackers where they want them and not allow them onto their inside shoulders.
- Players must communicate clearly.

VARIATIONS

Alter the position of the fullback and the covering defender; alter the number of attackers and defenders to create a 3v2 or 3v3 situation.

KICK CHASE DRILL

AGES: 14+

Skill execution: 3 • Decision making: 2 • Speed: 3

Agility: 2 • Endurance: 2 • Speed endurance: 2

OBJECTIVES

To develop the ability to execute a kick chase and defend the return; to practise the attacking kick return.

EQUIPMENT

One ball, four cones

SET-UP

Mark out a 25-by-25-metre to 40-by-40-metre grid with cones, depending on the age and skill level of your players. Split eight players into two groups of four. The defenders line up along one end line, and one of them has the ball. Two attacking players line up inside the grid, approximately three quarters of the way from where the kicker starts, ready to receive the ball. The other two attackers stand at the end line on either end of the defending line.

HOW TO PLAY

The player with the ball kicks it towards the two attackers in the grid. All the players are on side at the time of the kick. Once the ball is kicked, the defenders run towards the attackers in an organised line. The two attackers who receive the ball (normally winger[s] and fullback) attack the defenders for a specific number of tackles to try and score over the end line. The two attackers who were in the defensive line work hard to get back to give attacking options. Attackers and defenders switch roles after each specified number of tackles. The drill lasts for 5 to 10 minutes.

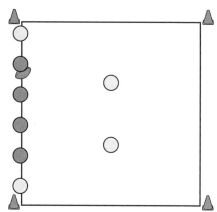

COACHING POINTS

- The player with the ball should strive for an accurate kick so that attackers can receive it easily.
- Defenders should chase the kick enthusiastically and in a well-organised manner.
- Attackers should make good use of space.

VARIATIONS

Alter the number of players in each group; the two attacking players who were in the defensive line start 10 metres nearer the other attackers.

KICKING-SPECIFIC 6V6V6

AGES: **14+**

Skill execution: 2 • Decision making: 3 • Speed: 3

Agility: 2 • Endurance: 2 • Speed endurance: 3

OBJECTIVES

To develop the organisation of a kick chase, kick reception, and decision-making skills.

EQUIPMENT

One ball, four cones

SET-UP

Mark out a 25-by-25-metre to 40-by-40-metre grid with cones, depending on the age and skill level of your players. Split players into three equal groups (groups A, B, and C). Groups A and C line up behind one another at one end of the grid. A player in the front group (group A) has the ball. The third group (group B) lines up near the opposite end, facing the other groups, ready to receive the ball.

HOW TO PLAY

Group A kicks the ball and chases the kick. Group B at the other end catches the ball and runs for one tackle. Group A jogs through to the far end, and group B goes back to its end and kicks the ball to group C, which is waiting at the other end. Group C catches the ball and runs for one tackle. Group B jogs through to the far end, and group C goes back to its end and kicks the ball to group A, who catches the ball and runs for one tackle. Play continues in this manner for 5 to 10 minutes.

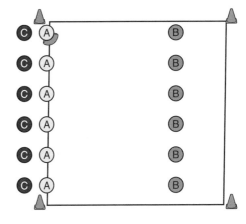

COACHING POINTS

- The player with the ball should strive for an accurate kick so the attackers can retrieve it easily.
- Defenders should chase the kick enthusiastically and in a well-organised manner.
- Attackers should make good use of space.

VARIATIONS

Set the receiving group in position to receive a kick as a back three would be in a game; allow the receiving group two or three tackles.

CHAPTER 5

Bag and Shield Drills

ag drills can be a useful tool in developing conditioning and communication skills because they tend to involve shuttle runs or getting up off the ground. The bags mimic this because, after tackling the bag, the player must get up from the ground. Bag drills can also be used as part of relays and for agility and jumping activities, both of which can add fun and variety to practice sessions. Many of the activities can be timed to add competition between groups.

However, note that bags are very rarely used when teaching actual tackle technique. Tackle technique should be practised player on player; shields or body armour can be used for body protection. When practising technique, a player holding a shield can move and use footwork to try to beat the tackler; a bag cannot.

If you are using bag drills with young players, be aware of the different maturity and fitness levels of your players, and organise them accordingly. Both maturity and fitness level will affect how well a player can get up off the ground. In addition, it is your duty to make sure that young players do not run from long distances and fly through the air to hit bags. Good tackle technique involves getting the feet close to the attacking ball carrier, and you should encourage this technique with both bags and shields.

Quality will completely go out the window if a player, particularly one lacking in basic fitness, is asked to move up and back and make 30 consecutive tackles. The number of tackles within each set should have a particular purpose and fitness goal. Rather than ask a rugby union forward to make 18 consecutive hits on a bag, mix a few hits with some grappling activity and work over the ball. Do not put your players through endless series of bag or shield drills, but intersperse these with more specific games and skill practices.

You may also want to combine handling skill activities with defensive bag or shield drills. These activities are easy to set up because they take up a small space and tend be in organised grids. They encourage players to switch from attack to defence and vice versa (e.g., switching from hitting tackle bags to immediately executing 3v2 decision-making drills). By having players carry out a physically demanding activity of driving or tackling bags or shields prior to performing a handling decision-making task, you can help them learn how to work when fatigued.

Combining attacking and defensive activities also adds interest to the session, facilitating learning. This approach can also be used for a whole session of mixing games with drills. Specific numbers of players are given in the drills but these are guidelines for the examples illustrated; you can alter the numbers in many cases to suit the group you are coaching.

ZIGZAG RUNS

AGES: ALL

Skill execution: 1 • Decision making: 0 • Speed: 2

Agility: 3 • Endurance: 2 • Speed endurance: 1

OBJECTIVES

To improve acceleration, deceleration, and change of direction.

EQUIPMENT

Eight tackle bags, one cone

SET-UP

Split players into groups of four to eight players. Tackle bags are lined up in two rows, approximately 2 metres apart. Players line up behind a cone that is approximately 2 metres from the first bag in one of the rows and face the bag.

HOW TO PLAY

The first player in line sprints forward to the first bag in the first row and then shuffles laterally around the first bag. The player then sprints forward to the second bag in the first row, and then shuffles laterally around the second bag, continuing in this manner through all of the bags.

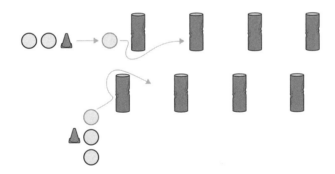

COACHING POINTS

- Players should get a fast start.
- Players should shorten their steps as they approach the bags.
- Players should maintain a good low body position (chest over knees over toes).

VARIATIONS

Allow players to fall to their chests on the bags, run or jump over the bags, or run or jump laterally over the bags; require players to run forward along the length of the bag and then laterally along the end and then backpedal down the length of the bag before shuffling to the next bag.

LEFT OR RIGHT ONE-ON-ONE

AGES: ALL

Skill execution: 1 ● Decision making: 1 ● Speed: 3

Agility: 4 ● Endurance: 1 ● Speed endurance: 2

OBJECTIVES

To practise speed off the line and changing direction and altering stride accordingly, particularly for on-line defence and for defence near the ruck in rugby union.

EQUIPMENT

Two shields per group, four cones

SET-UP

Split players into groups of three players; two players hold tackle shields and stand between 5 and 8 metres apart. The defender stands 3 to 5 metres from the shield holders.

HOW TO PLAY

The defender starts in a three-point stance and, on your command, moves forward approximately 2 metres with pace, at which point you signal one of shield holders to move forward and the defender moves to that shield to make a tackle. The defender must hold the shield holder tightly for three or four seconds and then rapidly realign into position. After the tackle, the defender takes over as the shield holder, and that shield holder now becomes the defender. The players work for a period of time or a certain number of tackles.

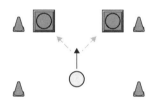

COACHING POINTS

- Defenders should move forward at pace for the first 2 metres and then shorten their stride length as they react to the shield holders moving forward.
- Defenders should keep their heads up and focus on the chest area of the shield holders.
- Defenders should get the front foot in a position close to the far foot of the shield holders so that they are close as they make shoulder contact with the shield.
- At contact, the defender locks the outside arm round the shield holder's body; the near arm will either go round the body or lift the near thigh, and the tackler's head will be in tight to the ball carrier's body.

VARIATIONS

Require the defenders to start on their chests (once they are proficient at the activity when standing); require shield holders to use specific footwork, such as stepping inside or outside (once they are more proficient, they can alter their lines more creatively).

LINE UNITY

AGES: ALL

Skill execution: 1 ● Decision making: 1 ● Speed: 2

Agility: 4 ● Endurance: 1 ● Speed endurance: 2

OBJECTIVES

To practise speed off the line, changing direction, and working together, particularly for on-line defence and for defence near the ruck in rugby union.

EQUIPMENT

Five tackle shields or tackle bags per group, four cones

SET-UP

Split players into groups of nine players. Five players line up 5 metres apart holding shields. Four players line up 3 metres away from the players holding shields and face them.

HOW TO PLAY

The defenders start in a three-point stance and, on your command, move forward 2 metres with pace, at which point you signal left or right, and the defenders move to that side to make the tackle. The defenders must hold the shield holder tightly for three or four seconds and then rapidly realign into position. After the tackle, the defender takes over for the shield holder just tackled, and that shield holder becomes a defender. The players work for a period of time or a certain number of tackles.

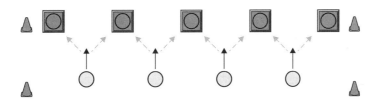

COACHING POINTS

- Defenders must use peripheral vision to be aware of the other defenders in the line.
- Players must communicate and work together as a defensive unit.
- Defenders should shorten their stride length as they change direction and approach the shield holders.
- After making good hits on the shields, the defenders should keep driving their legs to force the shield holders back.

VARIATION

Require the defenders to start on their chests (once they are proficient at the activity when standing).

Y DRILL

AGES: ALL

Skill execution: 1 ● Decision making: 1 ● Speed: 2

Agility: 4 ● Endurance: 1 ● Speed endurance: 2

OBJECTIVES

To practise speed off the line and changing direction in defence.

EQUIPMENT

Two tackle bags, two cones

SET-UP

Split players into groups of three. Two players hold bags and stand 5 to 8 metres apart, facing the third player, who stands at a cone 5 metres back from the bag holders and 3 metres in front of another cone.

HOW TO PLAY

On your command, the player at the cone (defender) turns and sprints to the back cone while still looking at the bags. At the second cone, the defender turns to return to the first cone; as the defender approaches the first cone, you signal one of the bag holders, and the defender moves to that side to make a tackle. The defender must hold the bag down for three or four seconds and then rapidly realign into position. After the tackle, the defender takes over as the bag holder, and the bag holder becomes the defender. The players work for a period of time or a certain number of tackles.

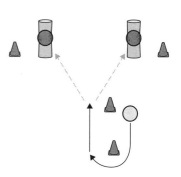

COACHING POINTS

- Defenders must keep the bag holders in sight while retreating to the cone.
- Defenders should move forward at pace for the first 2 metres and then shorten their stride length as they react to the bag holder moving forward.
- Defenders must keep their feet close to the bag as they make the hit.

VARIATIONS

Require defenders to start on their chests; have players use shields instead of bags; have players work in pairs (i.e., two defenders and two sets of two bags or shields).

ARC TO CONTACT

AGES: ALL

Skill execution: 1 ● Decision making: 0 ● Speed: 2

Agility: 2 ● Endurance: 2 ● Speed endurance: 2

OBJECTIVE

To practise putting the attacker to one side of the defender rather than allowing the attacker both sides to attack.

EQUIPMENT

Four tackle bags, four cones

SET-UP

Split players into groups of four. Four tackle bags are lined up 5 metres apart. Players line up 5 metres from the tackle bags.

HOW TO PLAY

On your command, the defenders move forward towards the bags, pointing at and naming the bags they are marking. The defenders move forward for two or three strides before arcing to one side of the bags and then stepping in to make a tackle. Defender must hold their bags down for three or four seconds before retreating by running forward (i.e., not back-pedalling), keeping their bag in sight. Defenders can then line up and repeat in the opposite direction. The players work for a period of time or a certain number of tackles.

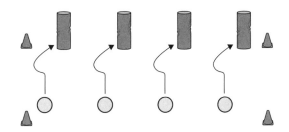

COACHING POINTS

- Defenders must take short steps (i.e., chop the stride) prior to contact, keeping their heads and hands up.
- Defenders should keep their heads close to the bags.

VARIATION

Require players to use a game-specific movement, such as a simulated pass from the breakdown as starting signal, before moving towards the bags.

BASIC SLIDE DRILL

AGES: ALL

Skill execution: 1 ● Decision making: 0 ● Speed: 2

Agility: 2 ● Endurance: 2 ● Speed endurance: 2

OBJECTIVES

To learn how to communicate as a group and slide together. Teams will use their own language for this movement (e.g., 'drift,' 'wedge,' etc.).

EQUIPMENT

Four tackle bags, four cones

SET-UP

Split players into groups of four. Four tackle bags are lined up 5 metres apart. The players line up 5 metres from the tackle bags and 2 metres off-centre.

HOW TO PLAY

On your command, the defenders move forward towards the bags, pointing at and naming the bags they are marking. The defenders move forward for two or three strides before sliding as a unit and then stepping in to make hits on the bags. The defenders must hold their bags down for three or four seconds before retreating by running forward, keeping their bags in sight. Defenders can then shuffle laterally to the starting position and repeat in the opposite direction. The players work for a period of time or a certain number of tackles.

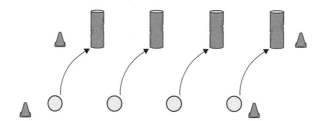

COACHING POINTS

- Defenders should line up on the inside of the bags with their inside shoulders.
- Defenders must take short steps prior to contact, keeping their heads and hands up.
- Defenders should keep their heads close to the bags.

VARIATION

Require players to use a game-specific movement, such as a simulated pass from the breakdown as starting signal, before moving towards the bags.

BACK AND MAINTAIN SHAPE

AGES: 12+

Skill execution: 1 ● Decision making: 0 ● Speed: 2

Agility: 2 ● Endurance: 2 ● Speed endurance: 2

OBJECTIVES

To practise speed off the line, changing direction, and working together in defence.

EQUIPMENT

Three tackle bags, three cones

SET-UP

Split players into groups of three. Three tackle bags are lined up 5 metres apart. The players line up 2 metres apart and next to a cone that is placed approximately 3 to 5 metres to one side of the tackle bags. These three players start on their chests. Two cones are placed 5 metres in front of the bags.

HOW TO PLAY

On your command, the defenders retreat by running back and then forward and through the two cones, maintaining their defensive shape, to tackle the bags. The players work for a period of time or a certain number of tackles.

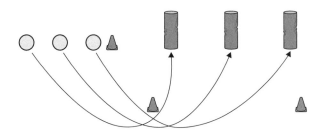

COACHING POINTS

- Defenders must get off the ground quickly.
- Defenders must run with their heads up around the cones and maintain their defensive shape.
- Individual players must not get in front of the defensive line.

VARIATIONS

Require players to use a game-specific movement such as a simulated pass from the breakdown as starting signal, before moving towards the bags; use four bags and indicate left or right as the players come forward through the cones so the group drifts as a unit in that direction.

SLIDE AND REALIGN

AGES: 12+

Skill execution: 1 ● Decision making: 0 ● Speed: 2

Agility: 2 ● Endurance: 3 ● Speed endurance: 3

OBJECTIVES
To learn how to slide together and communicate as a group.

EQUIPMENT
Four tackle bags, four tackle shields, ten cones

SET-UP
Split players into groups of 12. Four players stand 5 metres apart, holding tackle bags. Four players line up in front of cones that are 5 metres apart and 5 metres in front of the players holding the bags. Four players in another group hold tackle shields and line up 5 metres to the outside of the tackle bags and approximately 5 to 10 metres forward from the bags (the shield holders represent the next phase of play). Four more cones are placed 5 metres in front of the players with shields.

HOW TO PLAY
On your command, the four defenders move forward towards the players holding bags, pointing at and naming the bag holders they are marking. The defenders move forward for two or three strides before sliding as a unit and then stepping in to make hits on the bags. The defenders must hold the bags down for three or four seconds before retreating and running to the set of cones that are set up in front of the shield holders. When they reach these cones, they move forward and make hits on the shield holders. After the tackle, the defenders take the shields, the shield holders become bag holders, and the bag holders become defenders.

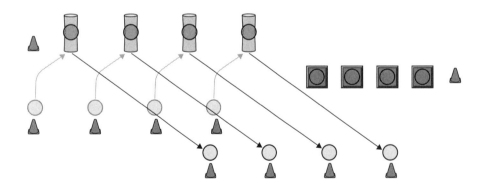

COACHING POINTS
- Defenders must communicate as a unit.
- Players must run with their heads up as they work to get back on side and maintain their defensive shape.
- Individual players must not get in front of the defensive line.

VARIATIONS
Require players to use a game-specific movement such as a simulated pass from the breakdown as starting signal, before moving towards the bags; replace the bags with shield holders, and replace the shield holders with players who receive the ball from the inside from a pass from the ground.

BAG TO SHIELD

AGES: 12+

Skill execution: 1 ● Decision making: 0 ● Speed: 2

Agility: 2 ● Endurance: 3 ● Speed endurance: 3

OBJECTIVE

To learn to work together as a defensive unit, especially when getting up from the ground.

EQUIPMENT

Four bags, four shields, two cones

SET-UP

Split players into groups of 16. Four players holding bags and four players holding shields line up 10 metres apart facing each other. Place two cones between the bag and shield holders. A group of four players lines up facing the bag holders, and another group of four players lines up facing the shield players.

HOW TO PLAY

On your command, both groups of defenders move forward towards the bags and shields, pointing at and naming the bags or shield holders they are marking. The defenders move forward for two or three strides before arcing to one side of the shields and then stepping in to make their hits. The defenders must drive their opponents (who offer resistance) for two or three seconds before retreating and running back to the set of cones to repeat the drill, this time facing the other direction (i.e., the defenders who tackled the bag holders now tackle the shield holders, and vice versa). The activity should last for a specific period of time or number of tackles.

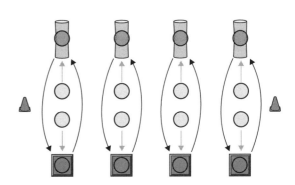

COACHING POINTS

- Defenders must keep the tackled players in sight while retreating to the cones.
- Defenders must communicate as a unit.

VARIATIONS

Require players to use a game-specific movement such as a simulated pass from the breakdown as starting signal, before moving towards the bags and shields; the players could tackle the bags and then lift them off the ground or above shoulder height.

HIT AND ADJUST

AGES: 12+

Skill execution: 1 ● Decision making: 0 ● Speed: 2

Agility: 2 ● Endurance: 3 ● Speed endurance: 3

OBJECTIVES

To practise adjusting position in defence after getting up from the ground; to learn how to work as a unit when fatigued.

EQUIPMENT

Four tackle bags and four tackle shields, four cones

SET-UP

Split players into groups of 12. Four players line up 5 metres apart holding tackle bags. Four players line up 5 metres from the tackle bags, facing them. Four other players hold tackle shields and line up 5 metres behind and between the bags.

HOW TO PLAY

On your command, the four defenders move forward towards the bags, pointing at and naming the bags they are marking. They move forward for two or three strides before arcing to one side of the bags and then stepping in to make their hits on the bags. The defenders must hold the bags down for three or four seconds before retreating (by running forward), keeping the bags in sight. At this time, the shield holders come through the gaps between the bags. (One shield holder will be outside the bags; decide whether you or the shield holders themselves will choose the side of the bags to run through.) As the shield holders come through the gaps, the defenders nominate which to hit, move forward, and slide onto their shields. The activity should last for a specific period of time or number of tackles.

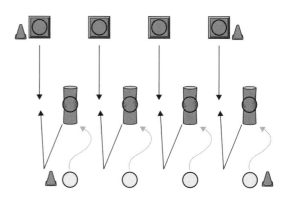

COACHING POINTS

- Defenders must communicate as a unit.
- Players must get up from the ground, quickly retreat, and realign as the defensive line.
- Players must use good footwork and shoulder contact when hitting the shields.

VARIATIONS

Require players to use a game-specific movement, such as a simulated pass from the breakdown as starting signal; allow the shield holders to leave some of the gaps empty and align themselves outside the bags, causing the defenders to have to communicate and slide.

DEFENSIVE CHOICE

AGES: 12+

Skill execution: 1 • Decision making: 1 • Speed: 2

Agility: 2 • Endurance: 3 • Speed endurance: 3

OBJECTIVES

To work on speed off the line, changing direction, and working together in defence.

EQUIPMENT

Eight tackle shields, four cones

SET-UP

Split players into groups of 12. Eight players line up 3 metres apart, holding shields (half of the shields are one colour and half are another; another option is to place a bib over one group of shields). Four other players line up 5 metres from the players holding shields, facing them.

HOW TO PLAY

On your command, all players move forward. When the shield holders have advanced 3 metres, call out one colour. The shields of this colour continue to move forward, and the others stop; the defenders must react both as individuals and as a unit and tackle the correct group of shields. The activity should last for a specific period of time or number of tackles.

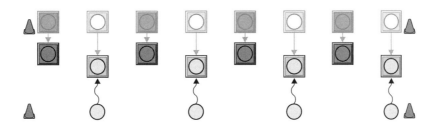

COACHING POINTS

- Shield holders should move forward quickly for the first 3 metres.
- Players should use good footwork, which is vital to chop the stride.
- Players must communicate well as a group.

VARIATIONS

Require that the defenders start on their chests or backs; require that the defenders start on their chests facing away from the shield holders.

NUMBERED BAGS

AGES: 12+

Skill execution: 1 ● Decision making: 0 ● Speed: 2

Agility: 2 ● Endurance: 2 ● Speed endurance: 2

OBJECTIVE
To learn how to maintain a defensive line.

EQUIPMENT
Six tackle bags, four cones

SET-UP
Split players into groups of twelve. Six players line up 5 metres apart and the other six players line up 3 to 10 metres from the tackle bags, facing them, depending on the age and ability level of the players. The players are numbered 1 through 6.

HOW TO PLAY
On your command, all players move forward, at which point you call out a number. Only the player whose number is called tackles a bag; the other players retreat to the starting line. The players move up again, and another nominated player makes the tackle and holds the bag down; the first player rises from the bag and retreats with the rest of the defensive line. The activity should last for a specific period of time or number of tackles.

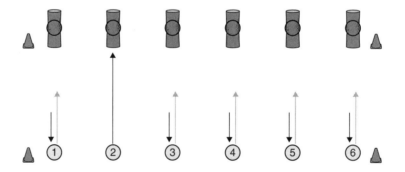

COACHING POINTS
- The defensive line should move forward quickly.
- Defenders should communicate well as a unit.
- Defenders should make good hits on the tackle bags.

VARIATIONS
Require the defenders to start on their chests at the beginning of each tackle; call out two numbers at once.

TWO-PLAYER NUMBER TACKLE

AGES: 13+

Skill execution: 1 ● Decision making: 1 ● Speed: 2

Agility: 2 ● Endurance: 2 ● Speed endurance: 2

OBJECTIVE

To learn how to work as a unit and execute two-person tackles.

EQUIPMENT

Six tackle bags, 10 cones

SET-UP

Split 18 players into three groups. Six players line up 5 metres apart holding tackle bags. The remaining players are divided into pairs and line up 5 metres from the tackle bags, facing them. Cones are placed 5 metres behind each pair.

HOW TO PLAY

On your command, the pairs of players move forward to the bags, but only the first pair tackles the bag using a 'one high, one low' approach (i.e., the first defender hits the bag at chest height and the second defender hits the bag lower down). The other players then retreat to the cones and back to the starting line, where the second pair makes the tackle and holds the bag down; the first pair rise up from the bag and retreats with the rest of the defensive line. The activity should last for a specific period of time or number of tackles.

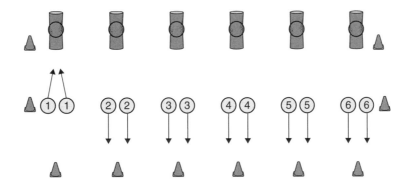

COACHING POINTS

- The hit from the two players should be almost simultaneous.
- Defenders must move forward together as a defensive unit.
- Each defender must talk to the defenders to the right and left to encourage them to move forward.

VARIATIONS

Call out two pairs at the same time; stagger the tackle bags to simulate an attacking line.

SIMULTANEOUS HITS

AGES: 14+

Skill execution: 1 ● Decision making: 1 ● Speed: 2

Agility: 2 ● Endurance: 2 ● Speed endurance: 2

OBJECTIVE
To practise continual marker defence for rugby league or back row for rugby union.

EQUIPMENT
Three tackle bags, four cones

SET-UP
Split players into groups of six. Three tackle bags are lined up 5 metres apart. The players are divided into pairs and lined up behind each other 5 metres from the tackle bags, facing them.

HOW TO PLAY
On your command, the first players from the first two lines move up and make a simultaneous hit on the second bag. The player coming from directly opposite the bag nominates the bag and tackles high; the player coming across chops the bag at the legs. The player who made the leg tackle gets up first and becomes the second (back) marker opposite the second bag. The player who made the high tackle gets up second and lines up as the first marker opposite the bag. On your signal, the first marker now moves across and chops the third bag as the player opposite the third bag makes a high tackle; the second marker holds the position and moves 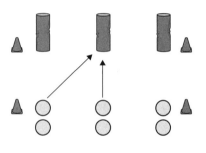 slightly to the blind side of the bag. When the end bag has been double tackled, the player who has stood up in the first marker position jogs around the back of the players to join the end of line 1, and the process restarts. The activity should last for a specific period of time or number of tackles.

COACHING POINTS
- Defenders must to work together to achieve a simultaneous hit on the bags, thereby doubling the impact force on the attacking player.
- Defenders must get their feet close to the bags when making their hits.
- Defenders must communicate who is tackling high and who is tackling low.

VARIATIONS
To simulate rugby league play, have the defenders keep their chests on the bags on the ground for four seconds before getting up; to simulate rugby union play, make the defenders roll away or get up quickly as if competing for the ball.

UP THE FIELD

AGES: 15+

Skill execution: 1 ● Decision making: 0 ● Speed: 2

Agility: 2 ● Endurance: 4 ● Speed endurance: 2

OBJECTIVES
To develop cardiorespiratory endurance, communication skills, and mental toughness.

EQUIPMENT
Four tackle bags, 10 cones

SET-UP
Split players into groups of eight. Four players line up 5 metres apart on the 10-metre line and hold tackle bags. The other four players line up on the 5-metre line, facing the players holding bags. Cones mark each line on the field.

HOW TO PLAY
On your command, the defenders move forward and tackle the bags. The defenders then retreat to the 5-metre line, and the bag holders move the bags back to the 15-metre line. The defenders then tackle the bags and retreat to the 10-metre line as the bags are moved back to the 20-metre line. This can take place all the way up the field. The activity should last for a specific period of time or number of tackles.

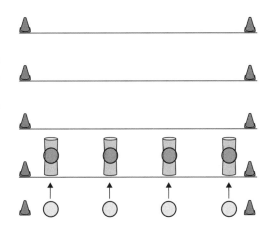

COACHING POINTS
- Defenders should move together.
- Defenders should communicate and nominate the bag holders.
- Defenders should practise getting their feet close to the bags and making good hits.
- Defenders should always get back onside.

VARIATIONS
After tackling the bag to the ground, the player jumps and picks the bag up; use tackle shields as opposed to tackle bags.

UP, READJUST, AND COVER

AGES: 14+

Skill execution: 1 ● Decision making: 0 ● Speed: 3

Agility: 2 ● Endurance: 3 ● Speed endurance: 3

OBJECTIVES

To learn how to readjust and mark the next attacking player after making the tackle by simulating the attacking team coming the same way after a breakdown; to practise maintaining the width of the defensive line.

EQUIPMENT

Six tackle bags, four cones

SET-UP

Split players into groups of eight or more. Six tackle bags are lined up 5 metres apart. Six players line up 5 metres from the tackle bags, facing them; two extra players line up behind each other at the first bag (there are two more defenders than bags to allow the end player time to get back to the first position).

HOW TO PLAY

On your command, the defenders move forward towards the bags, pointing at and naming the bags they are marking. The defenders move forward for two or three strides before arcing to one side of the bags and then stepping in to make their hits. The defenders must hold the bag down for three or four seconds before retreating to be opposite the next bag outwards in the line. The far defender sprints back to join the queue opposite the first bag. The activity should last for a specific period of time or number of tackles.

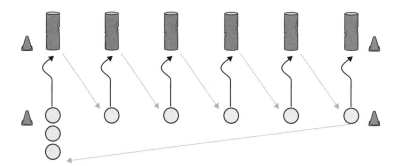

COACHING POINTS

- Defenders must communicate as a unit.
- Defenders must 'pull players out' to maintain the defensive width and ensure that there are equal numbers of defenders and attackers.

VARIATIONS

Require game-specific movements, such as a simulated pass from the breakdown as starting signal; require the final defender to sprint back a certain distance and round a cone prior to taking a place at the end of the first line.

INWARD ADJUST

AGES: 14+

Skill execution: 1 ● Decision making: 0 ● Speed: 2

Agility: 2 ● Endurance: 3 ● Speed endurance: 3

OBJECTIVE

To learn how to fill the tight spots near the breakdown.

EQUIPMENT

10 tackle bags, six cones

SET-UP

Split players into groups of 10. Ten tackle bags are lined up 5 metres apart. The players line up 5 metres from the tackle bags, facing them. Two cones are placed a minimum of 10 metres behind the middle two bags.

HOW TO PLAY

On your command, the defenders move forward towards the bags, pointing at and naming the bags they are marking. They move forward for two or three strides before arcing to one side of the bags and then stepping in to make their hits. The defenders must hold their bags down for three or four seconds; the two middle defenders sprint forward around the cone behind their tackle bags. They then line up opposite the last bag. The other players retreat to the starting position and move over one position so they are in front of the next bag in the line. The activity should last for a specific period of time or number of tackles.

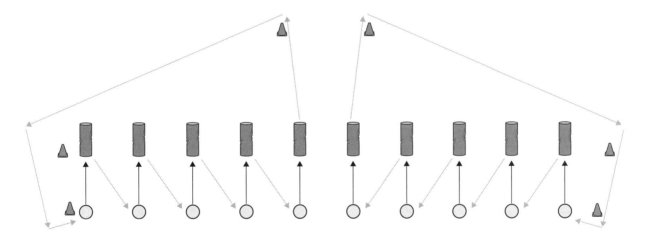

COACHING POINTS

- The two central bags represent the tight spots next to the breakdown, which must be adequately defended in a game.
- Defenders must keep the bags in sight while retreating to run again.
- Defenders must communicate as a unit and pull players in toward the ruck to cover the tight spot.

VARIATIONS

For younger players or more bags, start the activity with two players behind each other in a queue opposite the outside bags to give time for the runner to get around; require a game-specific movement, such as a simulated pass from the breakdown as starting signal.

ABC BAG DRILL

AGES: 15+

Skill execution: 1 ● Decision making: 0 ● Speed: 2

Agility: 2 ● Endurance: 4 ● Speed endurance: 4

OBJECTIVES

To improve cardiorespiratory endurance, willingness to work, and teamwork.

EQUIPMENT

Six tackle bags, six cones

SET-UP

Split up to 18 players into equal groups. Six tackle bags are lined up 5 metres apart. The players are divided into groups of three, and the players in each group line up behind each other 5 meters in front of a bag, facing it. Cones are placed 30 metres behind the players.

HOW TO PLAY

On your command, the first player in each group moves forward and tackles the bag; then retreats to the starting line. The first player makes six tackles in this manner and then sprints to the far cone and back. After the first player makes six tackles, the second player makes six tackles and then sprints to the far cone and back. Then, the third player does the same. After all three players in each line have had a turn, all three players in the group sprint together to the far cone and back. The sequence then starts again and continues for a specific period of time, but this time the second player starts first until the sequence is finished and then the third player starts first.

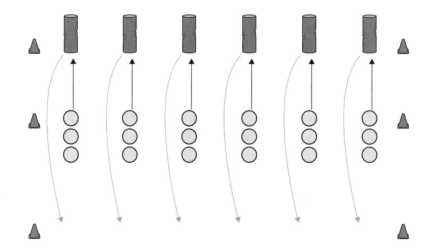

COACHING POINTS

- The defensive unit must move up together.
- Defenders must aim to get off their lines (i.e., move quickly for the first 2 or 3 metres).
- Defenders must get their feet close to the bags when making tackles.

VARIATIONS

Increase or decrease the required number of tackles; require the first player to make a tackle, then the second player, and then the third, continuing this sequence six times before running; require all the first players to tackle and then run as a group, continuing this sequence with the second and third players.

BREAK DRILL

AGES: 15+

Skill execution: 1 ● Decision making: 0 ● Speed: 2

Agility: 2 ● Endurance: 3 ● Speed endurance: 4

OBJECTIVE

To learn how to react to a line break.

EQUIPMENT

Six tackle bags, six tackle shields, eight cones

SET-UP

Split players into three groups of six. One group stands in a line 5 metres apart and holds tackle bags. Another group stands 30 metres from the players holding tackle bags; this group holds tackle shields. The remaining group stands 5 metres in front of the players holding tackle bags, facing them.

HOW TO PLAY

On your command, the defenders run forward and make tackles on the bags. On your next command, the defenders sprint back, simulating a break by realigning opposite the tackle shields. The defenders then make hits against the shields. The activity is carried out for a specific period of time or number of tackles.

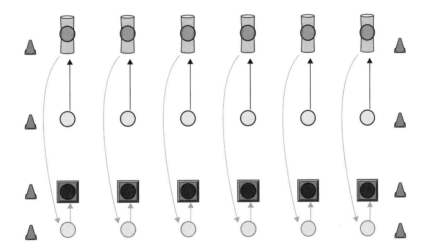

COACHING POINTS

- Defenders should move forward quickly for the first three strides.
- Defenders must use good footwork, which is vital to chop the stride.
- Defenders must communicate well as a unit.
- Defenders should sprint back with urgency.

VARIATIONS

Stagger the shield holders at various depths and widths to put more pressure on the integrity of the defensive unit; require the shield holders to use footwork to attempt to beat the defenders.

REALIGN AND DEFEND

AGES: 15+

Skill execution: 1 ● Decision making: 3 ● Speed: 3

Agility: 2 ● Endurance: 3 ● Speed endurance: 3

OBJECTIVES

To learn how to communicate as a group and work together to defend the situation at hand.

EQUIPMENT

Four tackle bags, seven cones, one ball

SET-UP

Split 16 players into two groups of four and one group of eight. Four tackle bags are placed 5 metres apart. Four players line up 5 metres from the tackle bags, facing them. The second group of four lines up behind these players. Two cones are placed 2 metres from one of the end players and are 1 metre apart (these represent the first two defenders from the ruck, guard, and bodyguard). Eight players line up as an attacking line on the other side of the two cones. An additional player stands by a cone placed beside the attacking line of players.

HOW TO PLAY

On your command, the first group of four defenders moves forward and makes a tackle on the bags before retreating and running around the two guard and bodyguard cones and line up approximately 5 meters apart opposite the live opposition. As the first group of defenders runs around the cones, the second group moves up to the starting position. On your command, the second group of defenders tackles the bags, and the first group moves up also as one defensive line for 5 metres. As the first group retreats, call a number; that number of players from the second group runs around the guard and bodyguard cones to join the first group of defenders, pushing the original defenders further out. On your command, the additional player with the ball (the scrum half) passes the ball to the attacking line. You determine the speed of the breakdown and the number of defenders. The numbers and the speed determine how the defenders defend against the attacking line. The activity is carried out for a specific period of time.

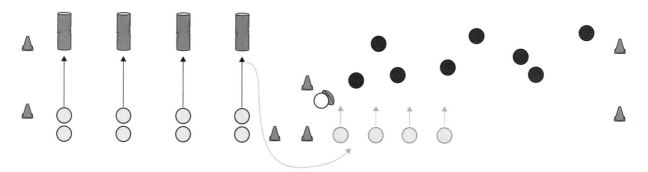

COACHING POINTS

- Defenders must adjust their width accordingly as more players join the defensive line.
- Defenders must communicate as a unit and defend according to the situation at hand.

VARIATION

Require a game specific-movement, such as a simulated pass from the breakdown as starting signal.

LIVE BREAK DRILL

AGES: 15+

Skill execution: 1 ● Decision making: 2 ● Speed: 2

Agility: 2 ● Endurance: 2 ● Speed endurance: 3

OBJECTIVE

To learn how to react to a line break and defend a live situation.

EQUIPMENT

Six tackle bags, nine cones, one ball

SET-UP

Split 18 players into three groups of six. One group of six stands 5 metres apart and holds tackle bags. Another group of six stands 5 metres in front of the players holding tackle bags, facing them. Three coloured cones are placed 30 to 60 metres behind the defenders, and the last group of six players stands in the space between, or off to the side of, these cones or one of these players has a ball.

HOW TO PLAY

On your command, the defenders move forward to tackle the bag holders. After a number of tackles, you call out a colour, and the defenders sprint back to that cone to defend a live play from that attack point (i.e., left-, right-, or centre-field). The attacking group lines up in an attacking formation with a scrum half nearest the nominated coloured cone. The scrum half passes the ball, and the attackers attack and attempt to break the defensive line with skilful play. The players who are sprinting back first will normally be instructed to sprint back to defend the breakdown as a priority. The activity is carried out for a specific period of time.

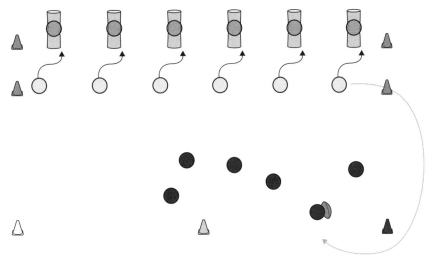

COACHING POINTS

- Defenders should move forward quickly for the first three strides.
- Defenders should us good footwork, which is vital to chop the stride.
- Players should communicate well as a group and work well as a unit.
- Defenders should sprint back with urgency.

VARIATIONS

Have players play more than one phase after the break (i.e., the attacking team plays for a set number of tackle, such as three or four, after the initial break); overload the number of players in the attacking group in order to make the defenders work harder.

CHAPTER 6

Non-Specific Rugby Games

The games in this chapter do not have rugby-specific rules; some are variations of other similar invasion games such as Australian rules and American football. They can be used as enjoyable conditioning activities particularly in the general preparation phase (early pre-season).

Developing rugby players need to play a wide variety of invasion games. Because rugby is a late specialisation sport, players should have a wide variety of skills and experience. Evidence suggests that players in key decision-making positions in elite rugby teams were good at other invasion games as youngsters. The games described in this chapter provide new stimulation and challenge players in ways that they may not experience in normal rugby games. In games such as soccer, basketball, and Australian football, the ball can be passed in many directions, unlike in rugby, in which the pass can be only lateral or behind. These games give players the chance to use more peripheral vision, which may facilitate cognitive development in a way that rugby does not.

Players who specialise too early, particularly in rugby union, may well miss out on key skills (e.g., a player pigeonholed as a lock from an early age may never practise kicking skills). The games described here give players the chance to practise some rugby skills they may not normally practise in their particular positions.

Many rugby-specific drills and games are small sided, which has the advantage of high player involvement. However, with the reduced numbers comes a smaller pitch, which can lead to players being comfortable only in small areas. Because of their nature, many of the passing and kicking invasion games that follow are played on quite a large pitch. The greater pitch size allows players to achieve maximum speed, which is not available to them in small grids, while also lessening the impact on the body as a result of fewer accelerations, decelerations, and direction changes. The larger pitch sizes and forward passes develop players' vision and communication skills over a greater area and through 360 degrees.

OFFSIDE TOUCH

AGES: ALL

Skill execution: 3 ● Decision making: 3 ● Speed: 3
Agility: 2 ● Endurance: 4 ● Speed endurance: 3

OBJECTIVES

To develop quick decision making using various passing (or kicking) options; to learn how to work off the ball and identify space.

EQUIPMENT

One ball, eight cones

SET-UP

Mark out a 20-by-30-metre to 40-by-60-metre grid with cones, depending on the age and skill level of your players. Set up two 5-metre scoring zones along both ends of the grid using cones and lines marked on the grid. Split 12 to 16 players into two equal teams. Players position inside the grid.

HOW TO PLAY

To begin the game, throw or bounce the ball into the centre of the grid. After a player has caught the ball, that player's team works together to pass the ball into the scoring zone using various passes up the field. The ball carrier may not move with the ball. The team in possession is allowed three touches (or fewer or more as you decide); otherwise, the other team gains possession. After being touched whilst in possession of the ball, a player must pass to a team-mate (this pass can be in any direction). If the ball goes to ground, you can either allow play to carry on or impose a turnover in which the opponent gains possession of the ball and play restarts from that location or a sideline. The game is played for a specific period of time, normally four to eight minutes.

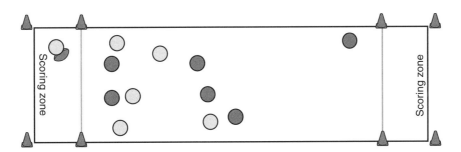

COACHING POINTS

- Players should strive for accurate passing and catching.
- Players off the ball should work hard to get into free space.
- Players should communicate well as a team.

VARIATIONS

Allow the ball carrier to hold the ball for only three seconds or to run with the ball only for a specific distance; after a score, require the scoring team to immediately attack the other end; on a turnover of possession, require that the team receiving the ball immediately attack the farther end; add player-on-player marking; require that the first pass must go forward and all other passes must go backwards (backwards pass after being touched); on the coach's whistle, the coach points to any side and then the team attacks that direction.

BIG CONE TOUCH

AGES: ALL

Skill execution: 3 • Decision making: 3 • Speed: 3

Agility: 2 • Endurance: 4 • Speed endurance: 2

OBJECTIVES

To develop quick decision making using various passing (or kicking) options; to learn how to work off the ball and identify space.

EQUIPMENT

One ball, 10 cones

SET-UP

Mark out a 20-by-40-metre to 40-by-60-metre grid, depending on the age and skill level of your players. Place cones on the corners of the grid and three large cones along each end line with a 3-metre exclusion zone around each. Split 16 to 20 players into two equal teams. Players position inside the grid.

HOW TO PLAY

To begin the game, throw or bounce the ball to the centre spot. After a player has caught the ball, that player's team passes or runs with the ball to touch one of the cones in its scoring zone. The team in possession is allowed two touches (or fewer or more as you decide) before it hands over possession; otherwise, the other team gains possession. After being touched whilst in possession of the ball, players must pass backwards to a team-mate; all subsequent passes can be in any direction. If the ball goes to ground, you can either allow play to carry on or impose a turnover in which the opponent gains possession of the ball and play restarts from that location or a sideline. The game is played for a specific period of time, normally four to eight minutes. After a score, the non-scoring team starts with the ball at the end line.

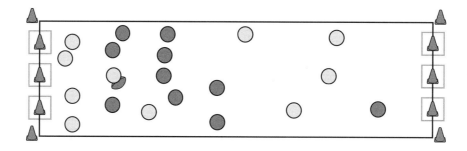

COACHING POINTS

- Players should strive for accurate passing and catching.
- Players should communicate well as a team.
- Players off the ball should work hard to get into free space.

VARIATIONS

Allow the ball carrier to hold the ball for only three seconds or to run with the ball only for a specific distance; after a score, require the scoring team to immediately attack the other end; on a turnover of possession, require that the team receiving the ball immediately attack the farther end; require at least two (or more, as you decide) legal rugby passes before a forward pass is allowed; add player-on player marking; require that the first pass must go forward and all other passes must go backwards.

TWO-TACKLE OFFSIDE TOUCH

AGES: 12+

Skill execution: 3 ● Decision making: 3 ● Speed: 3

Agility: 2 ● Endurance: 4 ● Speed endurance: 3

OBJECTIVES
To learn the concept of support play and to improve cardiorespiratory fitness.

EQUIPMENT
One ball, four cones

SET-UP
Mark out either a half-field or full-field area with cones, depending on the age, skill level, and number of players. Split 12 to 24 players into two equal teams. Both teams position around the field.

HOW TO PLAY
To begin the game, bounce the ball in the centre of the field. The team that catches the ball attacks its goal line. The ball carrier may run with the ball. The team in possession is allowed two touches before it hands over possession; otherwise, the other team gains possession. Players' first pass after being touched whilst in possession of the ball must go backwards; then, the team can attack using passes in any direction. After a turnover, the other team taps the ball to restart play and attacks the longest side. To score, a player must run with the ball over the goal line. The team that scores retains possession and attacks the opposite way. The game is played for a specific period of time, usually 5 to 10 minutes.

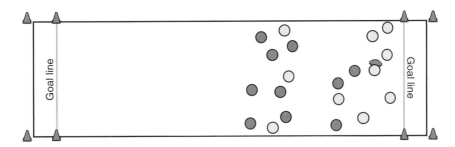

COACHING POINTS
- Attacking players must support the ball carrier and run into space.
- Ball carriers must choose the correct options and pass to players who are in space.

VARIATIONS
Require that ball carriers remain stationary; to give players a chance to recover, allow each team to have a target player who stands behind the goal line (the ball must be passed to this player to score, after which the player attacks in the other direction and is replaced by the player who passed the ball); use a player-on-player defence in which players can only tag their partners and vice versa; play as a kicking game using grubber and chip kicks (players may not run with the ball); require that all attackers be inside the 20/22-metre area within four seconds of the try being scored for the try to be awarded; require that by the time the score is awarded, all defenders must push inside the attacking half (otherwise, the other team scores double); on the coach's whistle, the coach points in any direction, and the team starts to attack that side.

AMERICAN TOUCH

AGES: 15+

Skill execution: 1 ● Decision making: 2 ● Speed: 4

Agility: 2 ● Endurance: 2 ● Speed endurance: 3

OBJECTIVES

To develop quick decision making using various passing (and kicking) options; to learn how to work off the ball and identify space.

EQUIPMENT

One ball, eight cones

SET-UP

Mark out a 20-by-50-metre to 50-by-100-metre grid with cones, depending on the age and skill level of your players. Set up two 5- to 10-metre scoring zones along both ends of the grid. Split 12 to 24 players into two equal teams. Players position inside the grid.

HOW TO PLAY

To begin, one team starts with the ball on the 20/22-metre line, and with a play-the-ball or snap of the ball, the ball goes from the ball carrier to another attacker. If a snap is used, the attacker who receives the ball is in the pocket and executes a forward pass. If a play-the-ball is used, the receiving attacker (the acting half) makes a rugby-style pass to another player, who, in turn, executes a forward pass. Each team has four downs, unless a score is made. Within one down or tackle sequence, the attacking team is allowed one forward pass from behind the original gain line and as many rugby passes as required before the ball carrier is touched. To score a touchdown, a player must run into, or pass to a player in, the scoring zone. On the third down or tackle, the team has the option of running the ball or kicking the ball to gain field position or to score a touchdown by being caught by a runner from the team (or to go for a drop goal if the larger grid size is used). On a touchdown, the opponents start with possession on their own 5-metre line. Teams are awarded six points for a touchdown and three points for a drop goal. You may wish to award one point for a conversion taken in front of the posts; in this case, the player who scored the touchdown will take the conversion. The game is played for a specific period of time, typically 5 to 15 minutes.

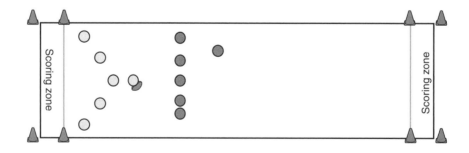

COACHING POINTS

- Players should strive for accurate passing and catching.
- Players off the ball should attempt to evade defending players and run into space.
- Players should communicate well as a team.

VARIATIONS

Allow only rugby-style passes in any direction and not one-handed forward passes; require that attacking teams must catch an onside kick to score a touchdown.

KICKBACK

AGES: 12+

Skill execution: 3 • Decision making: 2 • Speed: 0

Agility: 1 • Endurance: 1 • Speed endurance: 1

OBJECTIVES
To develop basic kicking and catching skills.

EQUIPMENT
One ball, four cones

SET-UP
Mark out either a half-field or full-field area with cones, depending on the age, skill level, and number of players. Split 12 to 24 players into equal teams. One team starts with the ball and positions on its 22- or 20-metre line, or one third of the way up the field when using a half pitch. The other team spreads out in the rest of the field.

HOW TO PLAY
The team with the ball must try to kick it out over the sidelines in the opponents' half of the field, with a bounce within the field of play. In league play, extra points are awarded for 40/20s (i.e., the ball is kicked from inside the player's own 40-metre zone but bounces into touch in the opponents' 20-metre zone; bounces in the field of play but crosses the touch line within 20 metres of the goal line), or for getting the ball to rest in the in-goal area. In union play, extra points are awarded for getting the ball off field within 10 metres of the opponents' goal line. In union play, if the ball alights in goal, the opponents restart on the 22-metre line, and if the ball goes dead, they restart on the centre field on the halfway line. In league play, if the ball goes dead, the opponents start with the ball on the 20-metre line. Opponents who catch the ball after it has bounced must kick it from where they caught it. Opponents who catch the ball before it bounces must walk forward 10 metres before kicking it. If the player attempting to catch the ball knocks the ball forward with the hands or arms so that it touches the ground, the other team is awarded a point. If the ball is kicked out on the full, the other team gains possession and restarts play in the centre of the field. The game is played for a specific period of time, usually between 5 and 10 minutes.

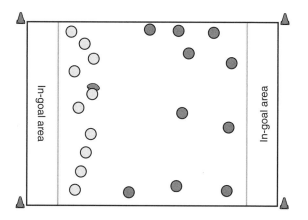

COACHING POINTS
- Players should strive to use good kicking and catching techniques.
- Players receiving the kick must communicate with each other so that the appropriate player catches the ball.

VARIATIONS

Add one or two more balls when working with larger groups of players or players with higher skill levels; enforce additional penalties (e.g., a player who knocks the ball on is out of the game, or a player who knocks the ball loses 10 metres); allow attacking players who catch the ball on the full the option of passing backwards to a team-mate in a better kicking position; give receiving players the option of running the ball in a counterattack where, upon catching the kick, the catcher holds the ball in the air and shouts 'Run,' and the team has six plays in which to score (normal touch rules apply, but the team that runs loses its right to kick; a team cannot use the running option on consecutive kick receptions).

ONSIDE SOCCBY

AGES: 11+

Skill execution: 2 ● Decision making: 2 ● Speed: 3

Agility: 2 ● Endurance: 4 ● Speed endurance: 2

OBJECTIVES

To learn how to quickly organise an attack after receiving the ball and to quickly organise a defence from a very erratic position.

EQUIPMENT

One soccer ball, eight cones

SET-UP

Mark out either a half-field or full-field area with cones, depending on the age, skill level, and number of players. Split 12 to 24 players into equal teams. The game is played with a soccer ball.

HOW TO PLAY

The game starts with a kick-off from the centre spot, and normal soccer rules apply. However, if a player catches the ball on the full, that player's team then plays on for three touches in which normal touch rugby rules apply. On the third touch, the ball is dropped and neither the defender nor the attacker involved in that last play is allowed to touch the ball; whoever gets to the ball first starts the game again using soccer rules. The same rule applies if a ball is passed forward or knocked on. If a team scores a try (four or five points), or a soccer goal (one point), the player who scored kicks the ball out from the ground at the goal and the teams attack the opposite end. The game is played for periods of 10 to 15 minutes and is primarily used in the pre-season.

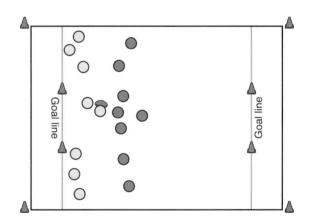

COACHING POINTS

- The team that catches the ball on the full must react quickly and get into onside positions to attack.
- Offside defenders must work hard to get back onside and defend as a unit.

VARIATIONS

Play the game using a rugby ball; alter the number of tackles; limit the number of tackles in possession to one before a turnover takes place (however, players who catch the ball on the full may pass it by hand or kick it to a team-mate in any direction); have a defender kick the ball out after a goal is scored in which case the teams continue to attack the same end for the rest of the game.

AUSSIE RULES

AGES: 12+

Skill execution: 3 ● Decision making: 2 ● Speed: 3

Agility: 3 ● Endurance: 4 ● Speed endurance: 3

OBJECTIVES

To develop quick decision making using various passing (and kicking) options; to learn how to work off the ball and identify space.

EQUIPMENT

One ball, four cones

SET-UP

Mark out a 30-by-50-metre to 50-by-100-metre grid with cones, depending on the age and skill level of your players. Set up three 5- by-10-metre scoring zones along each end of the grid, with an inner high-scoring zone and two outer low-scoring zones. Split 12 to 24 players into two equal teams.

HOW TO PLAY

To begin the game, throw or bounce the ball on the centre spot, or have one team start with possession on its goal line. Players hand pass (i.e., punch the end of the ball) or kick the ball to one another in any direction. A

player who catches the ball on the full from a team-mate's kick may call 'Mark,' and the opponents must retreat 10 metres to allow the player a free kick. Players may run no more than 10 metres before they must pass or kick the ball. Player who are touched in possession must immediately kick or pass; otherwise, the ball is turned over. Teams score using kicks through the scoring zones along the end line (six points for kicking the ball through the high-scoring zone and one point for kicking through the low-scoring zones).

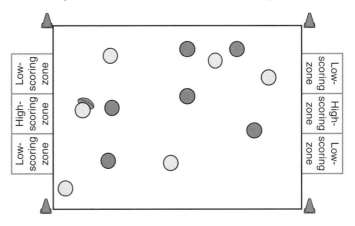

COACHING POINTS

- Players must work off the ball and get into space.
- Ball carriers must look for team-mates who are available and in good space.
- Players should try to execute accurate kicks and exhibit good catching skills.

VARIATIONS

Alter the distance players may move with the ball; require the defenders to grip the ball carrier to effect a touch; only allow scoring from inside the 20/22-metre line nearest the end in which the point is to be scored.

AUSSIE TACKLE-TOUCH

AGES: 12+

Skill execution: 3 ● Decision making: 3 ● Speed: 3

Agility: 3 ● Endurance: 3 ● Speed endurance: 3

OBJECTIVES

To develop quick decision making using various passing (and kicking) options; to learn how to work off the ball and identify space; player realignment.

EQUIPMENT

One ball, four cones

SET-UP

Mark out a 30-by-50-metre to 50-by-100-metre grid with cones, depending on the age and skill level of your players. Split 12 to 24 players into two equal teams. Players position throughout the pitch.

HOW TO PLAY

To begin the game, throw or bounce the ball on the centre spot, or have one team start with possession on its goal line. Players hand pass (i.e., punch the end of the ball) or kick the ball to one another in any direction. Players who catch the ball on the full from a team-mate's kick may call 'Mark' and the opponents must retreat 10 metres to allow the player a free kick. A try is scored by running the ball into the end zone either after marking a kick or in the subsequent running phase. Played with a rugby ball, normal Aussie rules apply, but if players catch the ball on the full (i.e., mark), they can play on for two touches with normal touch rugby rules applying. If a player decides to run with the ball, he must indicate by holding the ball in the air and shouting "Run." After the second touch, the ball is dropped and neither the defender nor the attacker involved in that last play is allowed to touch the ball; whoever gets to the ball first starts the game again with Aussie rules. The same rule applies for forward passes and knocks on. The direction of each team's attack changes every three or four minutes after a brief rest.

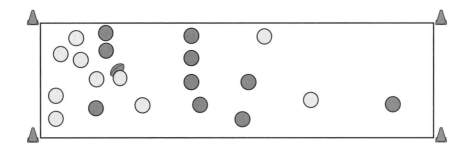

COACHING POINTS

- Players must work off the ball and identify space.
- Players should use accurate kicks and good jumping and catching techniques.
- Once the ball has been caught on the full, the attacking team must create good attacking options and support the ball carrier.

VARIATION

Require that players may call the mark only from a kick from their own team or from a kick from either side.

CHAPTER 7

Small-Sided Rugby Games

The games outlined in this chapter are for a small number of people, usually eight or fewer per side. They tend to work on passing accuracy, attacking and defensive decision making, plus communication and support play. They are suitable as warm-up games for adults and as main games for younger and less experienced players.

Small-sided games have been used as a coaching tool for a number of years in many sports; they are also primarily what children play. A small group of children can be seen in a park, on a street, or at school with a ball playing a game of football (any code), basketball, or cricket. They have made their own pitch and modified the laws of the international game to suit their own needs, which are generally enjoyment, participation, and equality.

Small-sided games provide a greater level of participation because they allow players to carry the ball many more times than they would in a full-sided game. In addition, players also get to act as close supporters more often, and are constantly challenged to make decisions in both attack and defence. Small-sided games not only expose young players to more challenging situations than drills do, making them more enjoyable, but also lead to better cognitive development. They often address a specific aspect, or microcosm, of the larger game to put pressure on players' skills and decision-making processes.

The games in this book are described primarily as touch games, but you can adjust the level of contact to suit your players' needs. The games vary in intensity, but most, if not all, would be suitable as conditioning games. If you are using the games as a conditioning tool, be aware of the importance of planning and observation. You should carefully monitor the amount of time your players are in play, the pitch dimensions, and individual participation to ensure that the work-to-rest ratios are appropriate and that each player is placed under adequate physical stress. It is important that a player does not "loiter" in a position to avoid work. It is also important that in games, such as 6v3 + 3 where there is an imbalance in skill between the groups, that this does not mean that a particular group only rarely defends due to the other side losing possession too easily.

Also keep in mind that the games outlined here are quite stressful physically because they require a lot of acceleration, deceleration, and changes of direction. You should also be aware that using these games alone is not sufficient running fitness training. One component of running fitness is maximum speed, which is an important part of the game for outside backs; the small pitch size and general lack of an adequate rolling start in these games results in outside backs never achieving the speed they would in the game. Allied to this is the lack of long-distance speed endurance training that outside backs would encounter, for example, in repeated kick-and-chase and counterattack situations.

COLOUR CONE TOUCH

AGES: 14+

Skill execution: 3 ● **Decision making: 3** ● **Speed: 2**

Agility: 4 ● **Endurance: 3** ● **Speed endurance: 2**

OBJECTIVES

For attacking players to make quick decisions and identify available space; to practise defensive realignment and communication.

EQUIPMENT

Three or four balls, 24 cones

SET-UP

Mark out a 20-by-25-metre to 30-by-40-metre grid, depending on the age and skill level of your players. Place coloured cones around the edges of the grid. Split 10 to 14 players into two equal teams. The defending team starts with the ball, and each defensive player is assigned a colour.

HOW TO PLAY

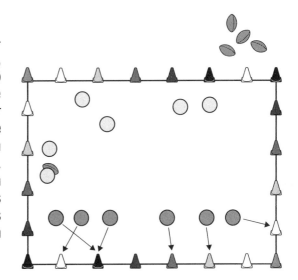

The game is played under normal touch rules with you deciding on the method and speed of the breakdown. To begin, the defending team drop-kicks the ball from its own line to the attacking team. When an attacking player is touched, the defensive players must run around the nearest cone of their nominated colours before they can re-enter the defensive line. If an attacking player makes an error, the attacking team must run back and collect another ball from behind its line. Normal rugby scoring rules apply (i.e., the attacking team scores by placing the ball on or behind the defending team's goal line). The attacking team has a set number of plays (normally between three and six) or a set period of time in possession of the ball.

COACHING POINTS

- Attackers must be able to identify space and move the ball quickly.
- Attackers must be able to exploit advantages in numbers and exploit 2v1 situations.
- Defenders must work to get back quickly and communicate to recreate an effective defensive line.

VARIATION

If cones are limited, number players instead. When a number is called, players with that number lie on the floor and do not re-enter the defensive line until the next play, or at each breakdown the players with a certain number retreat to a particular corner or area.

PARRAMATTA TOUCH

AGES: 14+

Skill execution: 3 • Decision making: 3 • Speed: 3

Agility: 2 • Endurance: 3 • Speed endurance: 3

OBJECTIVES

For attacking players to make quick decisions and identify available space; to practise defensive realignment and communication.

EQUIPMENT

One ball, 10 cones

SET-UP

Mark out a 20-by-30-metre to 30-by-40-metre grid, depending on the age and skill level of your players. Create a centre line of cones and set up two 10-metre zones at each end of the grid. Split 12 to 18 players into three equal groups. One group is the attacking team and lines up across the centre line with the ball. The other two groups are defending teams, and each team lines up inside the two 10-metre zones.

HOW TO PLAY

To begin, the attackers attack one of the defensive zones and have one tackle in which to score. If the attacking team scores a try, the defenders must run around the centre cones and get back to their defensive zone, after which the attackers can start attacking again from the central line. The defenders are not allowed to leave their defensive zone (i.e., they must stay behind the 10-metre cones when the attacking team has the ball). If the attackers fail to score as a result of a tackle or handling error, they immediately turn around and attack the other set of defenders. This continues for a set period of time or for a set number of attacks.

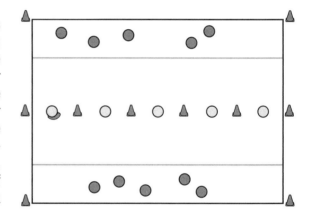

COACHING POINTS

- Attackers must be able to identify space and move the ball quickly.
- Attackers must be able to exploit advantages in numbers and exploit 2v1 situations.
- Defenders must work to get back quickly and communicate to recreate an effective defensive line.

VARIATIONS

To encourage attacking success, increase the number of attackers so there is an overload; require the defenders to hold tackle shields.

QUICK BALL TOUCH

AGES: 14+

Skill execution: 3 ● Decision making: 3 ● Speed: 1

Agility: 2 ● Endurance: 4 ● Speed endurance: 2

OBJECTIVES

For attacking players to practise making quick decisions and supporting the ball carrier.

EQUIPMENT

One ball, four cones

SET-UP

Mark out a 30-by-40-metre to 40-by-60-metre grid with cones, depending on the age and skill level of your players. Split 12 to 18 players into two equal teams. Both teams start near the centre of the grid.

HOW TO PLAY

To begin, one team kicks the ball from the centre line. Normal touch rules apply. The defence will be between 3 and 7 metres back from the position of the tackle (also called the advantage line or offside line). There is no breakdown; instead, players who are touched must immediately pass to a team-mate or turn the ball over. Attacking players must pass from where they were touched. The attacking team is allowed six tackles in possession of the ball. Kicking is not allowed. After the sixth tackle, the player puts the ball down and immediately retreats with the rest of the team to the offside line, and the other team picks up the ball and starts to attack. Normal rugby scoring rules apply (i.e., the attacking team scores by placing the ball on or behind the defending team's goal line). The game lasts for a specific period of time, typically three to five minutes.

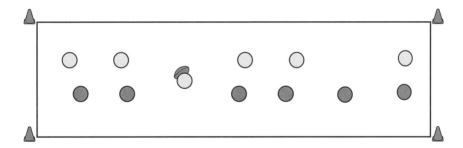

COACHING POINTS

- Attackers must be able to identify space and move the ball quickly.
- Attackers must be able to exploit advantages in numbers and exploit 2v1 situations.
- Attackers must support the ball carrier.
- Defenders must work to get back quickly and communicate to recreate an effective defensive line.

VARIATIONS

Require touched players to drop to the floor and get up before passing the ball; require touched players to immediately scoop the ball through their legs and to a supporting player, who must catch the ball before it hits the ground (if not caught, the ball is turned over).

SCATTERED DEFENCE

AGES: 14+

Skill execution: 3 ● Decision making: 3 ● Speed: 2

Agility: 4 ● Endurance: 3 ● Speed endurance: 3

OBJECTIVES

For attackers to practise making quick decisions and communicating to realign; for defenders to practise getting back quickly into position when not conventionally aligned.

EQUIPMENT

Ten balls, up to 28 cones

SET-UP

Mark out a 25-by-30-metre to 30-by-40-metre grid, depending on the age and skill level of your players. Each end line is made up of cones of different colours (at least four different colours). Behind each end line are five balls, numbered 1 through 5. Split 12 to 18 players into two equal teams (attackers and defenders). Each player is identified with a colour; more than one player can have the same colour. Both teams start near the centre of the grid.

HOW TO PLAY

To begin the game, call a number. All attackers run to their end line and around the ball of that number before one of them picks the ball up to play. At the same time, defenders run back to their end line and go onto their chests at a cone of their nominated colour. They then get up and try to stop the attackers. Normal touch rules apply. The attackers have one tackle in which to score. If the team scores, the players immediately turn around and attack the other end of the grid when all attacking players having crossed the goal line; in this case the defenders must turn and retreat to their particular colour at the far end of the grid before turning to defend. If the attacking team is touched in possession, you call a number and the team that was defending retreats to pick up that ball as per the start. Players on the team that was attacking turn and sprint to the cones of their nominated colours, where they go to ground. Replace the balls in their original positions as they are used. The game is played for a set period of time, usually three minutes.

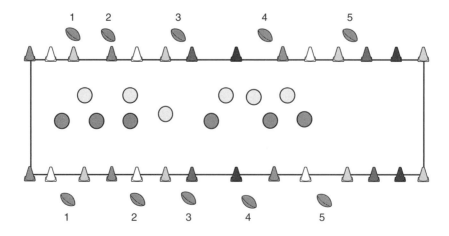

COACHING POINTS

- Attackers must be able to identify space and move the ball quickly.
- Attackers must be able to exploit advantages in numbers and exploit 2v1 situations.
- Attackers must work hard to get into an effective attacking shape.
- Defenders must work to get back quickly and communicate to recreate an effective defensive line.

VARIATIONS

Increase the number of tackles allowed to score; allow one team to continually attack until all five balls are used.

SMALL-SIDE OFFSIDE TOUCH

AGES: 14+

Skill execution: 3 ● Decision making: 3 ● Speed: 3

Agility: 3 ● Endurance: 3 ● Speed endurance: 2

OBJECTIVE

For attacking players to practise getting into and passing into available space; for defenders to practise anticipating the movements of the attackers.

EQUIPMENT

One ball, four cones

SET-UP

Mark out a 35-by-50-metre grid with cones. Split 10 players into two equal teams. Four attackers and three defenders start in the grid. Remaining players are at one sideline as interchange players.

HOW TO PLAY

Pass or kick the ball to start play. The attacking team tries to score by passing to a player beyond the far goal line, after which it immediately turns and attacks the other end. A player from the attacking team who is touched in possession places the ball on the ground. After the touch, two players from what was the attacking team run to the sideline and are replaced by the spare player from their team; one player from the defending team leaves the field and is immediately replaced by the two team-mates on the sideline. This player swapping reverses the 4v3 situation, so that the other team is now attacking. When the players have swapped, a player from the team that is now attacking picks up the ball (no defender can challenge until this player has passed or run 5 metres). The game is played for a set period of time, usually five minutes.

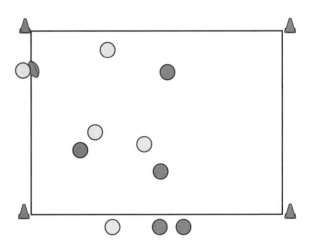

COACHING POINTS

- Attackers must pass the ball accurately.
- Attackers must be able to identify space and move the ball quickly.
- Attackers must work hard to get into effective attacking positions.

VARIATIONS

Increase the number of tackles allowed; do not allow the attackers to run with the ball; play rugby rules, allowing only lateral and backward passes.

6V3+3

AGES: 14+

Skill execution: 3 ● Decision making: 3 ● Speed: 3

Agility: 2 ● Endurance: 3 ● Speed endurance: 3

OBJECTIVES

For attacking players to practise making quick decisions and executing accurate passes; for defenders to learn to work effectively when short of numbers.

EQUIPMENT

One ball, six cones

SET-UP

Mark out a 30-by-40-metre grid with cones and place a cone in the centre of each goal line. Split 12 players into two equal groups. Six attackers start with the ball on one goal line, and three defenders position on the opposite goal line at the other end of the grid. The remaining three defenders are on the sideline or goal line as interchange players.

HOW TO PLAY

On your command, the attackers attack the opposite goal line. When the attacking team scores or makes a handling error, players must sprint back and around the central cone on their goal line. At this time, the three original defenders step out of the grid, and the three interchange players step in. After running around the cone, the attackers now attack the three new defenders. You decide how many phases each group of three players has to defend; the attackers will normally have a maximum of four tackles in which to score against each set of three players. The game is played for a set period of time, usually five minutes, or a set number of attacks for each team.

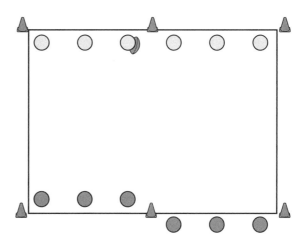

COACHING POINTS

- Attackers must pass the ball accurately.
- Attackers must be able to identify space and move the ball quickly.
- Attackers must work hard to get in effective attacking positions.

VARIATION

If the attacking teams has the ball for more than one phase (tackle), require attacking players who are touched to go to ground and make the ball available either by playing the ball or by good presentation (the defence will retreat a distance you have chosen).

ONE-TACKLE TOUCH

AGES: 14+

Skill execution: 3 ● Decision making: 3 ● Speed: 1

Agility: 4 ● Endurance: 4 ● Speed endurance: 2

OBJECTIVES

To learn how to transition from attack to defence and vice versa; to learn how to make quick decisions, identify space, make short, accurate passes while fatigued, and run the correct lines.

EQUIPMENT

One ball, four cones

SET-UP

Mark out a 5-by-15-metre to 5-by-25-metre grid with cones, depending on the age and skill level of your players. Split six to eight players into two equal groups (attackers and defenders). The attackers start with the ball on one goal line, and the defenders position on the opposite goal line at the other end of the grid.

HOW TO PLAY

On your command, the attackers attack the opposite goal line. If they score, drop the ball, or keep possession but fail to score, they immediately put the ball down and the other team attacks, but the new defenders must first get back to their goal line before they are onside to defend. The game lasts for a specific period of time, normally between 30 and 60 seconds.

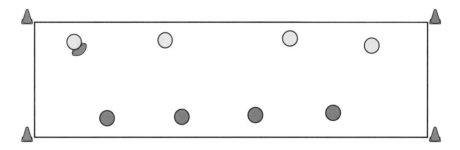

COACHING POINTS

- Players should use accurate passes.
- Players should have the ability to successfully execute a 2v1 situation.

VARIATION

For an uneven number of players, give the attackers an advantage (e.g., players on the attacking side who score or are touched in possession must put the ball down and immediately join the other team so that the new attacking side has the advantage).

KILLER TOUCH

AGES: 15+

Skill execution: 2 ● Decision making: 2 ● Speed: 3

Agility: 2 ● Endurance: 4 ● Speed endurance: 4

OBJECTIVES

To learn decision-making skills in both attack and defence while fatigued.

EQUIPMENT

One ball, four cones

SET-UP

Mark out a 10-by-20-metre to 30-by-40-metre grid with cones, depending on the age and skill level of your players. Split 8 to 16 players into two equal teams. The attackers start with the ball on one goal line, and the defenders are on the opposite goal line.

HOW TO PLAY

On your command, the attackers attack the opposite goal line. Normal touch rules apply. The attacking team gets one play in which to score. If the attackers score, they stay in possession and both teams swap sides, restarting play from the goal lines. If a player is touched, the ball is placed on the ground and the entire team sprints back to its goal line and then becomes the defending team. The new attackers immediately restart the game with a tap or a play-the-ball with at least one pass from the breakdown before play continues. The game is played for a specific period of time, typically between one and three minutes.

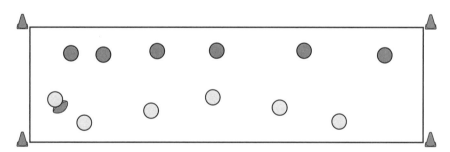

COACHING POINTS

- Attackers must exploit the disorganised defenders and create gaps.
- Defenders must work hard to get back and defend.
- All players must be able to mentally switch from offence to defence, and vice versa, quickly.

VARIATION

After a player in possession is touched, require both teams to retreat to their respective lines before coming back for the restart (the defence positions 5 metres from the restart spot).

GRID 4V3

AGES: 12+

Skill execution: 3 • Decision making: 3 • Speed: 1

Agility: 3 • Endurance: 3 • Speed endurance: 2

OBJECTIVES

For defenders to learn to work as a unit and communicate while fatigued; for attackers to learn how to fix or drag a defender, identify space, make short, accurate passes, and run the correct lines.

EQUIPMENT

One ball, four cones

SET-UP

Mark out a 10-by-20-metre to 15-by-20-metre grid with cones, depending on the age and skill level of your players. Split seven players into two teams (four attackers and three defenders). The attackers start on one goal line, and the defenders are on the opposite goal line.

HOW TO PLAY

To begin, you or a player on the defending team grubber kicks the ball to the attackers. The attackers attack the opposite goal line. When a player is touched, defenders retreat the 5 metres, and the attacker who was touched restarts play by tapping the ball with her or his foot. The game lasts for a specific period of time, normally between one and three minutes, or a specific number of tackles.

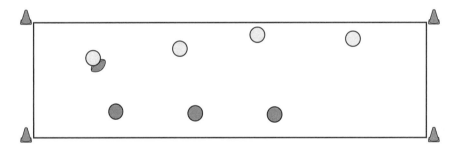

COACHING POINTS

- Defenders must maintain their defensive alignment and not jump the line.
- Support runners must work hard off the ball to create space.
- Support runners must run good attacking lines.

VARIATIONS

To make the activity more physically demanding, require the defenders to go onto their chests at each tackle; require the defenders to retreat to the back line before they are onside to encourage attackers to play to the advantage line.

CONTINUOUS 4V3

AGES: 14+

Skill execution: 3 ● Decision making: 3 ● Speed: 1

Agility: 3 ● Endurance: 2 ● Speed endurance: 2

OBJECTIVES

For defenders to practise working as a unit and communicating while fatigued; for attackers to learn how to fix or drag a defender, identify space, make short, accurate passes, and run the correct lines.

EQUIPMENT

One ball, four cones

SET-UP

Mark out a grid that is 15 to 20 metres wide by 30 to 50 metres long with cones. Split seven players into two teams (four attackers and three defenders). The attackers start on one goal line, and the defenders are 3 to 5 metres back.

HOW TO PLAY

On your command, the attackers attack the opposite goal line. When a player is touched, the defenders retreat the required distance (normally 3 to 5 metres), and the attackers restart with the touched player tapping the ball with his foot. An attacking player who breaks through may run between 5 and 10 metres (your choice) before being called to stop; the defenders sprint back and realign. At the end of the grid, the defenders swap places with some of the attackers, and the new attacking team realigns and attacks the other way. The game lasts for a specific period of time, normally between two and four minutes.

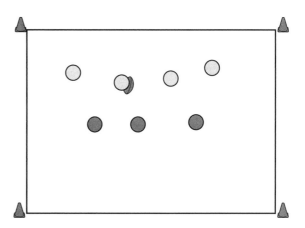

COACHING POINTS

- Defensive players must maintain their defensive alignment and refrain from jumping the line.
- Attacking players must try to fix defenders to create a 2v1 situation.

VARIATIONS

Require defenders to go onto their chests at each tackle (you must control the speed of the restart; for example, 1, 2, 3 play); increase the number of attackers to five.

INTERVAL BALLS

AGES: 12+

Skill execution: 3 • Decision making: 3 • Speed: 2

Agility: 2 • Endurance: 3 • Speed endurance: 2

OBJECTIVES

For defenders to practise working as a unit and communicating while fatigued; for attackers to learn how to fix or drag a defender, identify space, make short, accurate passes, run the correct lines and use appropriately-weighted kicks.

EQUIPMENT

Five balls, 12 cones

SET-UP

Mark out a 30-by-30-metre to 30-by-40-metre grid with cones, depending on the age and skill level of your players. Split 16 players into two equal teams (or you can have a slight overload on the attack). Place four cones along the side of the grid at 5-metre intervals from the goal line with one ball next to each one. The attackers start at the end of the grid at the 25-metre line; one player has a ball. The defenders start 3 to 7 metres behind the attacking player with the ball.

HOW TO PLAY

The game starts with an onside pass from the ground at the sideline at 25 metres by the attackers (you control the speed of the restart). The attackers attempt to score by crossing the ball over the defender's goal line; they have four tackles in which to score. The attackers will most likely use an attacking kick on one of their possessions to score. When the first score is made using the ball from the 25-metre line, the attackers immediately sprint back and line up onside at the 20-metre mark and again have four tackles in which to score using the ball at that line. Play continues in this manner until all the balls on the sideline are used. If the team fails to score or get the kick away, it forfeits possession. When all the balls have been used, the teams switch.

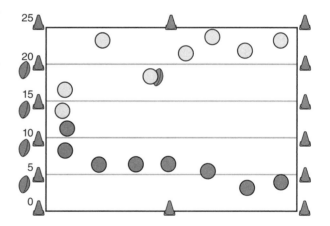

COACHING POINTS

- The support runners must maintain running options to engage the defenders, thus creating space for the kick.
- The ball carrier must choose good attacking options.
- The attacking players must anticipate a kick from the ball carrier and react accordingly.

VARIATIONS

Alter the number of tackles in each set (i.e., use a pyramid style in which the number decreases on each play, such as 5, 4, 3, 2, 1); place several balls at each marker, and if a team scores on that specific attack (e.g., from the 25-metre line), it has another attack from that line, until it fails to score from that cone or uses up all the balls, whichever comes first; require defenders to go onto their chests at each tackle (you must control the speed of the restart).

SMALL-SIDED THREE-ZONE DEFENCE

AGES: 14+

Skill execution: 3 ● Decision making: 2 ● Speed: 2

Agility: 2 ● Endurance: 3 ● Speed endurance: 2

OBJECTIVES

For attackers to learn how to exploit overloads, particularly on the short side; to learn decision making and how to hold or fix defenders and execute accurate passes.

EQUIPMENT

One ball, eight cones

SET-UP

Mark out a 20-by-30-metre grid with two 5-metre zones along the sides. Split 11 players into two teams (seven attackers and four defenders). The attackers position on their goal line with a ball, and the defenders position 5 to 10 metres back. Two defenders are restricted to the central zone, and one defender is in each outside zone (attackers may move anywhere).

HOW TO PLAY

To begin, you or the defenders kick the ball out from the goal line. The attack has three tackles in which to score. A player can be tackled with a two-handed touch, after which the game is restarted with a tap. Attacking players who are tackled in the outside zone must tap and pass the ball back into the central zone. Kicking is not allowed. The team scores by placing the ball over the opponents' goal line. The game is played for a specific period of time, typically between one and three minutes.

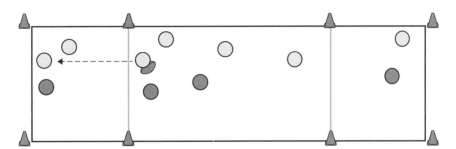

COACHING POINTS

- Ball carriers must fix defenders to create space and a 2v1 situation in the outside channel.
- The ball carrier must execute accurate passes in the outside channel to exploit the 2v1 situation.

VARIATIONS

Add a defender to one of the outside zones; require the defenders to retreat to the goal line on each occasion (you decide whether the ball has to be passed back into the central zone after a tackle in the outside zone, depending on the attackers' ability); when the ball is moved into the outside zone, allow the defender nearest to this zone to move into this zone and the far defender to move into the central zone.

6V4 ROTATION

AGES: 11+

Skill execution: 3 ● Decision making: 3 ● Speed: 3

Agility: 2 ● Endurance: 4 ● Speed endurance: 2

OBJECTIVES

To develop the ability to fix or drag a defender and make quick decisions and short, accurate passes; to learn how to work off the ball, identify space, and run the correct lines; for defenders to practise working as a unit and communicating while fatigued.

EQUIPMENT

One ball, four cones

SET-UP

Mark out a 20-by-40-metre to 20-by-60-metre grid with cones, depending on the age and skill level of your players. Split players into teams of 10 (six attackers and four defenders). The attackers position at one end of the grid along their goal line. The defenders start at the other end of the grid.

HOW TO PLAY

To begin the game, put the ball into play or have a defender kick the ball to the attackers. On receiving the ball, the attackers attack the defenders. When a player is touched, the defenders retreat a required distance (usually 5 to 7 metres), and the attackers restart with the touched player tapping the ball with her or his foot and then passing the ball to another attacking player. The game lasts for a specific period of time, normally between one and three minutes, or a specific number of tackles. After the specific time or number of tackles, two defenders swap with two attackers.

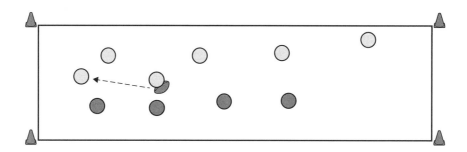

COACHING POINTS

- Defenders must maintain their defensive alignment and not jump the line.
- Attackers must choose the correct options and execute 2v1 plays.

VARIATION

Require defenders to go onto their chests at each tackle (you must control the speed of the restart).

SMALL-SIDED RUCK DEFENCE

AGES: 13+

Skill execution: 3 ● Decision making: 1 ● Speed: 1

Agility: 3 ● Endurance: 2 ● Speed endurance: 2

OBJECTIVE

To learn defensive organisation around the play-the-ball or ruck area.

EQUIPMENT

One ball, four cones

SET-UP

Mark out a grid that is 50 metres long (i.e., between the 20-metre lines in rugby league and the 22-metre lines in rugby union) and is 20 to 30 metres wide. Split 11 or 15 players into two teams (six defenders and five attackers for league, or eight defenders and seven attackers for union). The attackers start with the ball 5 metres from the end line.

HOW TO PLAY

To begin, the ball carrier taps the ball and runs forward or passes the ball to another player. In league play, when the attacking player is touched, the markers get set in the correct place while the other defenders retreat the required distance, tie in to the required width from the tackle, and number off (to make sure that the attackers do not have extra players at one side of the tackle). The first defender from the tackle may call 'A,' and the second may call 'B.' When touched, attacking players go onto their chests, then their backs, and over to their chests (not a roll) before playing the ball. If you blow your whistle on the touch, the attacker must drop to the ground chest down and execute a quick play-the-ball. The game is played for a specific period of time, typically one to three minutes, or for a predetermined number of tackles (usually 6 to 18 depending on the age and skill level of the players).

In union play, when the attacking player is touched, the two nearest defenders go to their chests while the other defenders retreat a required distance and number off and nominate guards and bodyguards. When touched, the attacking player goes to ground and makes the ball available; the two nearest attackers mark the defenders who are on their chests. If you blow your whistle on the touch, this indicates a slow ball and the ball is not passed from the breakdown until you indicate. The attacking team has the ball for many tackles (e.g., 18) or for a specific period of time, normally between 90 seconds and three minutes, unless it loses possession.

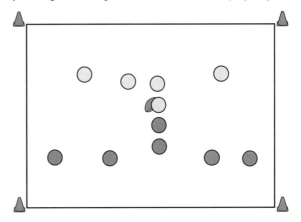

COACHING POINTS

- Defensive players must communicate well.
- Defenders must number off either side of the breakdown and adjust their width according to the width of the attack.

VARIATIONS

Require the markers or guards to go to their chests at the breakdown; require all defenders or attackers to go to their chests; play using full or controlled contact.

INSIDE-OUTSIDE DEFENCE

AGES: 14+

Skill execution: 3 ● Decision making: 4 ● Speed: 2

Agility: 3 ● Endurance: 4 ● Speed endurance: 2

OBJECTIVES

To learn defensive systems and how to adjust them according to the position of the attack; to practise working as a unit and communicating while fatigued.

EQUIPMENT

One ball, four cones, one set of tags

SET-UP

Mark out a 20-by-30-metre to 30-by-50-metre grid with cones, depending on the age and skill level of your players. Split 10 players into two equal teams (attackers and defenders). The defenders are at one end of the grid. The attackers are wearing tags and start in the field of play.

HOW TO PLAY

To begin the game, put the ball into play or have a defender kick the ball to the attackers. On receiving the ball, the attackers attack the defenders. Attackers are considered tackled when their tags are removed according to one of the following:

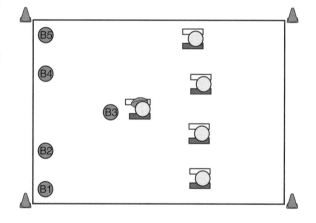

- *Out-to-in defence:* A defender must remove an attacker's outside tag to effect a tackle. Note that in this diagram, the defenders are using an out-to-in defence. B3 has made the tackle; if the attackers run straight, B1 and B2 would remove the darker tags, and B4 and B5 would remove the lighter tags.

- *In-to-out defence:* A defender must remove the inside tag to effect a tackle.

The game is restarted with a tap and one defender opposite the attacker with the ball. With larger numbers of players, the ball will be played rugby league style or presented rugby union style; in either case, two defenders will be committed to the breakdown as markers or guards. The game lasts for a specific period of time, normally between one and three minutes, or for a specific number of tackles. After the specific time or tackle number, two defenders swap with two attackers.

COACHING POINTS

- Defenders must maintain their alignment and number off either side of the breakdown.
- Attackers must be able to choose the correct options and create and execute 2v1 plays.

VARIATION

Require defenders to go onto their chests at each tackle (you must control the speed of the restart).

TOUCH OVERLOAD

AGES: 10+

Skill execution: 3 • Decision making: 3 • Speed: 3

Agility: 2 • Endurance: 4 • Speed endurance: 2

OBJECTIVES

To develop the ability to fix or drag a defender and make quick decisions and accurate passes; to learn how to work off the ball, identify space, and run the correct lines; for defenders to practise working as a unit and communicating while fatigued.

EQUIPMENT

One ball, four cones

SET-UP

Mark out a 30-by-40-metre grid with cones. Split 12 players into two equal teams. The six attackers position in the field of play. Three defenders position on the other goal line, and the remaining three defenders position outside the grid behind the line.

HOW TO PLAY

To begin the game, put the ball into play or have a defender drop-kick the ball to the attackers. When a player is touched, the defenders retreat a required distance and the attackers restart with the touched player playing the ball with his or her foot. The defending team must have one marker, or guard, at the breakdown. The attacking team is allowed six tackles with the ball. At the end of each series of tackles, whether a score occurs or not, another defender is added to the defending team. The game lasts for the specific number of sets (e.g., 6v3, 6v4, 6v5, 6v6). Play is typically a total of 10 to 15 minutes. If the attacking team makes an error (e.g. drops the ball), it loses either that particular set of tackles or all its sets, your choice.

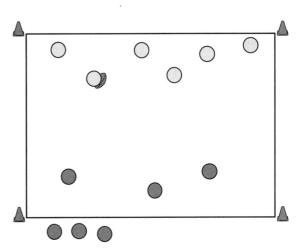

COACHING POINTS

- Attackers must try to create scoring opportunities.
- Defenders must work hard as a unit and use the appropriate defensive system for the situation depending on the number of players.

VARIATION

Allow only three tackles in which to score; require players who make tackles to go to their chests; require all defenders to go to their chests after a tackle; allow the attackers the same number of tackles as there are defenders (e.g., if there are three defenders, the attackers get three tackles).

DEFENDERS DOWN

AGES: 15+

Skill execution: 3 ● Decision making: 3 ● Speed: 3

Agility: 2 ● Endurance: 4 ● Speed endurance: 2

OBJECTIVE
To learn how to make decisions in defence while under fatigue.

EQUIPMENT
One ball, four cones

SET-UP
Mark out a 20-by-40-metre grid with cones. Split 16 players into two equal teams. The eight attackers position on their goal line with a ball. Five defenders position 5 metres back from the attackers, and the remaining three defenders start on their chests at the advantage line.

HOW TO PLAY
To begin, the attackers play the ball. The attacking team has six tackles in which to score. When ball carriers are touched, they go onto their chests, then their backs, and then their chests (not a roll) before playing the ball. There are no markers. The defenders who were at the advantage line may not defend until they are back onside. At each tackle, three defenders must go onto their chests at the advantage line. The attacking team has three sets with the ball. When a try is scored, the attackers all get behind the goal line and attack the other way. If the attackers make an infringement, they start again from the starting position. Each team has two or three minutes in possession.

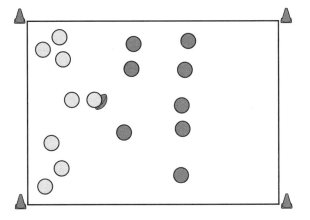

COACHING POINTS
- Attackers must be able to execute 2v1 situations.
- Defenders at the advantage line must work hard to get back onside.
- Defenders must communicate well and work as a unit.

VARIATIONS
Number the defenders so they go down in order (e.g., players 1, 2, and 3 at tackle 1; players 4, 5, and 6 at tackle 2); require the attackers to score within a set period of time (e.g., two minutes).

8V8 TRANSITION GAME

AGES: 15+

Skill execution: 3 ● Decision making: 4 ● Speed: 3

Agility: 2 ● Endurance: 3 ● Speed endurance: 2

OBJECTIVES

To develop quick decision making using various passing and kicking options and learn how to go from a line defence system to an offside attack and vice versa; to learn how to work off the ball and identify space.

EQUIPMENT

One ball, four cones

SET-UP

Mark out a 40-by-40-metre to 50-by-60-metre grid with cones, depending on the age and skill level of your players. Split 16 players into two teams. The attackers (team A) position near their goal line, and the defenders (team B) position 5 metres back from the attackers.

HOW TO PLAY

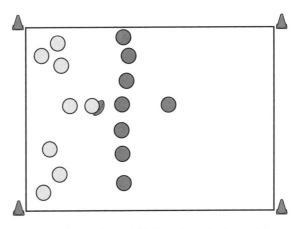

To begin, team A taps or plays the ball. The attacking team's first pass must be backwards or lateral, after which any number of forward passes are allowed within each tackle sequence. The attackers are allowed three (or fewer) touches before they must turn the ball over. Team B restarts with a play-the-ball, is allowed no forward passes, and has six tackles in which to score. Team B can play the ball immediately on the turnover even though some of the attackers will be in offside positions. Team B must work to get back onside; they may not effect a touch until they have come from an onside position. If a player in an offside position touches a player, the tackle count goes back to zero. The game is two-handed touch (between the thigh and chest), and kicking is not allowed. You determine the speed of the play-the-ball. The game is played for blocks of time, usually three to eight minutes.

COACHING POINTS

- Players must strive to use accurate passes and catches.
- Players must work well off the ball and communicate with each other.
- The offside team should work back to become defenders.
- Attackers must try to exploit chaotic defensive systems.

VARIATIONS

Allow only rugby-style passes; allow the attacking team to use kicks.

THREE-TEAM ROTATIONAL TOUCH

AGES: 11+

Skill execution: 3 ● Decision making: 3 ● Speed: 2

Agility: 2 ● Endurance: 3 ● Speed endurance: 2

OBJECTIVES

To develop the ability to fix or drag a defender and make quick decisions and short, accurate passes; to learn how to work off the ball, identify space, and run the correct lines; for defenders to practise working as a unit and communicating while fatigued.

EQUIPMENT

One ball, four cones

SET-UP

Mark out a 20-by-40-metre to 40-by-60-metre grid with cones, depending on the age and skill level of your players. Split 18 players into three teams (two attacking teams and one defending team). One attacking team positions at the end of the grid with the ball. The other attacking team positions outside the grid at the opposite end. The defending team positions 5 metres back from the attacking team with the ball.

HOW TO PLAY

The attackers attack the defenders. When a player is touched, the defenders retreat a required distance, and the attackers restart with the touched player tapping the ball with her or his foot or playing or rolling it to another player. The game lasts for a specific period of time, normally between one and three minutes, or for a specific number of tackles. Kicking is not allowed. At the end of the set, the defenders rest, the attacking team defends, and the resting team attacks. During the second attack, the resting team (previously the defending team) jogs to the other end of the grid to prepare to become attackers in the third set. With a two-minute attack, players work for four minutes and rest for two.

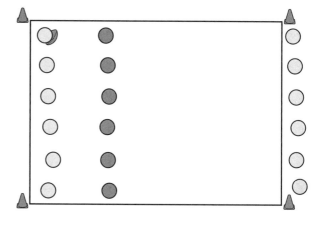

COACHING POINTS

- Defenders must maintain their defensive alignment and number off at either side of the breakdown.
- Attackers must try to hold and drag defenders out of position to create space.

VARIATION

Require the defenders to go onto their chests at each tackle (you must control the speed of the restart).

PLAYER-ON-PLAYER TOUCH

AGES: 10+

Skill execution: 3 ● Decision making: 2 ● Speed: 3

Agility: 3 ● Endurance: 4 ● Speed endurance: 2

OBJECTIVES

To develop quick decision making and communication using various passing options; to learn how to work off the ball, identify space, and develop defensive awareness.

EQUIPMENT

One ball, four cones

SET-UP

Mark out a 30-by-60-metre grid. Split players into two teams of six to ten players. Each player is paired with a player on the opposite team.

HOW TO PLAY

To begin, the defenders kick the ball to the attackers. Ball carriers who are touched must go onto their chests, roll onto their backs, and then go back the other way onto their chests before playing the ball. The game is two-handed touch (between the thigh and chest), and kicking is not allowed. The team in possession has six tackles with the ball. Attacking players can only be touched by the opposing players they are paired with. After a score, the attacking team restarts with a play on the 5-metre line and attacks in the other direction. All players must be onside at this point; otherwise, the team turns over possession.

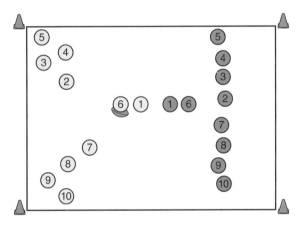

COACHING POINTS

- Attacking players should try to lose their opponents by making good use of the space available and moving rapidly from one part of the attacking line to another.
- Attacking players must move about and create space by losing their defenders.
- Attacking players must call for the ball when they see an opportunity.

VARIATION

Allow a specified number of rugby-style forward passes per tackle phase.

DEFENSIVE DRIFT

AGES: ALL

Skill execution: 3 ● Decision making: 3 ● Speed: 2

Agility: 2 ● Endurance: 4 ● Speed endurance: 2

OBJECTIVES

To develop the ability to fix or drag a defender and make quick decisions and accurate passes; to learn how to work off the ball, identify space, and run the correct lines; for defenders to practise working as a unit and communicating while fatigued.

EQUIPMENT

Up to 12 balls, four cones

SET-UP

Mark out a 30-by-40-metre to 40-by-50-metre grid with cones, depending on the age and skill level of your players. Split 14 players into two teams (eight attackers and six defenders). The defenders position on the goal line, and the attackers position in the field of play.

HOW TO PLAY

To begin, the attackers receive the ball from you or from the defenders via a drop kick. When a player is touched, the defenders retreat a required distance and the attackers restart with the touched player playing the ball with his foot. When an infringement occurs, the attackers sprint back behind the start line and immediately collect another ball from a corner to attack (all attackers must get behind this line before the ball can be played). If a player scores, all attacking players must get behind the goal line before the team turns and attacks the other way. The attacking team has unlimited tackles with the ball. The game lasts for a specific period of time, typically two or three minutes.

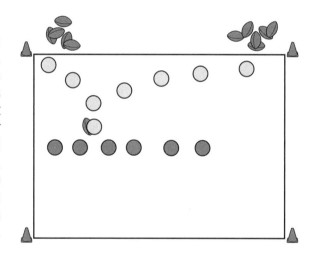

COACHING POINTS

- Defenders must communicate and work together as a unit.
- Defenders must not come out of the defensive line.
- Attacking players must create space and run appropriate attacking lines rather than just chain pass along the line.

VARIATIONS

Require the guards, or markers (the two defenders nearest the tackle), to go to their chests at the breakdown; require tackled players to go to their chests, then their backs, and then their chests (not a roll); require all of the defenders to go to their chests.

CHAPTER 8

Large-Sided Rugby Games

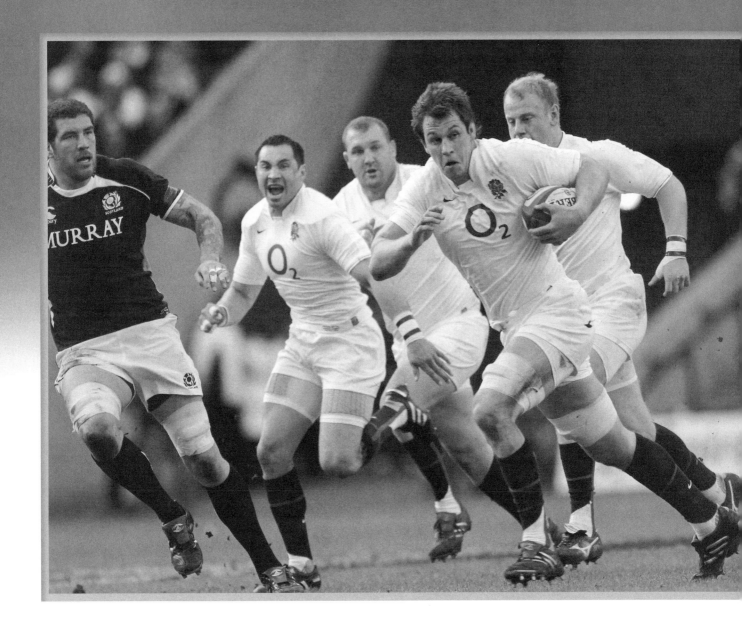

The games outlined in this chapter are for a large number of people, usually nine or more per side. They work on passing accuracy, attacking and defensive decision making, communication, and support play. They also work on attacking shape, offload decisions, and strategic kicking. Each game highlights the key areas of transition from attack to defence and vice versa. Attacking and defensive organisation are also covered. These games are not generally suitable as warm-up games, but are used for adults and youth players as main games. The games vary in intensity, but most, if not all, would be suitable as conditioning games.

The main purpose of larger rugby-specific games is to create, develop, and test various aspects of team tactics and decision making. It is up to you to develop your own games depending on the particular tactics and aspects of play you believe your players need to work on. These games are particularly useful in developing the general attacking shape of the team and playmakers' ability to take the team around the field. In particular areas of the field, the games test the key decision makers and support runners.

Some of the games (Offload Touch, Shield Offload Option, Fast Ball) can be used to develop particular types of play (e.g., a fast offload and support game, a game around flat attack). Because the games in this chapter concentrate more on the big picture, they are more appropriate for higher-end youth and adult teams and less appropriate for younger players. If you use them with younger players or players of lesser ability, use them sparingly and concentrate mostly on smaller-sided and non-specific games. With higher-skilled youth and adult teams, you could still use them in conjunction with small-sided games and drills as part of a whole-part-whole approach.

THREE-COLOUR TEAM TOUCH

AGES: 14+

Skill execution: 3 ● Decision making: 3 ● Speed: 3

Agility: 2 ● Endurance: 4 ● Speed endurance: 2

OBJECTIVE

To improve decision making in attack and defence under pressure.

EQUIPMENT

One ball, four cones

SET-UP

Mark out a 40-by-40-metre to 60-by-70-metre grid with cones, depending on the age and skill level of your players. Split 18 to 24 players into two teams (attackers and defenders). Then split the defending team into three teams and give each team an identifying number or colour. The defending team starts behind the goal line. The attacking team starts in the field of play.

HOW TO PLAY

To begin, the defending team kicks the ball to the attacking team. Normal touch rules apply, and you dictate the speed and conditions of the breakdown. After the first tackle is made, call the number or colour of one of the defensive subsections; these players must retreat behind their own goal line and take no further part in the game. The attacking team has a set number of tackles or period of time, usually one to three minutes, in which to score as many points as possible.

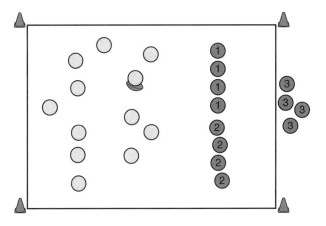

COACHING POINTS

- Defenders must communicate well and work as a unit.
- Attacking players must choose the correct support options.
- Ball carriers must fix or drag defenders.

VARIATIONS

Require the defenders to go to ground; allow the non-participating defensive group to rejoin the game after retreating behind the goal line, and have another section retreat at the next tackle.

KICK CHASE TOUCH

AGES: 15+

Skill execution: 3 • Decision making: 4 • Speed: 4

Agility: 2 • Endurance: 3 • Speed endurance: 4

OBJECTIVES
To improve the kick chase and decision making in attack.

EQUIPMENT
One ball, 10 cones

SET-UP
Mark out a 40-by-50-metre to 70-by-100-metre grid with cones, depending on the age and skill level of your players. Mark the 22-metre and 10-metre lines (union) or 20-metre and 40-metre lines (league) with cones. Split a minimum of 18 players into two teams. The defenders start at the halfway line, and the attackers start in the field of play in front of their goal line.

HOW TO PLAY
To begin, the defending team kicks the ball out from the halfway line as in restarting the game after a score. Normal touch rules apply, with you dictating the speed and conditions of the breakdown. The attacking team has a set number of tackles (normally six) in possession and must kick on the last tackle. The attacking team scores tries as per the rules of the game. After kicking the ball, the attacking team becomes the defensive team and is awarded one point each time it tackles a player in the opposition's 20- or 22-metre area (e.g. if the team makes four consecutive tackles in the 20- or 22-metre area, it scores four points). If the team kicks the ball from inside its own 40-metre area into touch in the opposition's 20- to

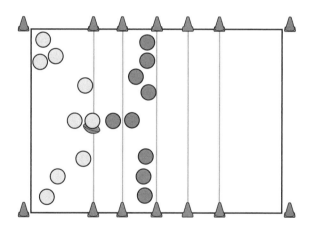

22-metre area after bouncing in the field of play, it regains possession and has another set of tackles in which to score. When a team is kicking on the last tackle of this tackle set, normal rules of the full international game apply. After a try is scored, the other team kicks off from the halfway line as per the rules of the game.

COACHING POINTS
- Defenders must communicate well and work as a unit to put pressure on the kicker.
- Defenders must retreat well and get behind the ball to return it from their own 20- or 22-metre area.
- Attacking players must choose the correct support options and set up a good kick chase.

VARIATION
After a try has been scored, the scoring player kicks the ball out from the goal line to the opponents and then runs out to join team-mates in the field of play to put them onside before they then move forward as a kick chase team and become the defensive line.

OUT OF THE 22

AGES: 15+

Skill execution: 3 ● Decision making: 4 ● Speed: 4

Agility: 2 ● Endurance: 2 ● Speed endurance: 3

OBJECTIVES

To improve the kick chase and decision making in attack (this game is more applicable to rugby union but could be used in rugby league to improve hard yardage gains).

EQUIPMENT

One ball, 10 cones

SET-UP

Mark out a 40-by-60-metre to 70-by-100-metre grid with cones, depending on the age and skill level of your players, with the 22-metre line (union) or 20-metre lines (league) marked with cones. Split a minimum of 18 players into two teams. The defenders start at the halfway line, and the attackers start in the field of play in front of their goal line.

HOW TO PLAY

To begin, the defending team kicks the ball out from the halfway line as in restarting the game after a score. Normal touch rules apply with you dictating the speed and conditions of the breakdown. The attacking team has a set number of tackles in possession depending on its field position and must kick on the last tackle. The attacking team has the following restrictions:

- Two tackles in its own 22-metre zone
- Four tackles between its 22-metre line and the halfway line
- Six tackles between the halfway line and its opponents' 22-metre line
- Eight tackles in the opponents' 22-metre zone

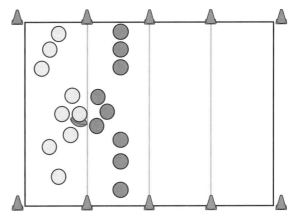

If the attacking team gets into the next zone within the required number of tackles, the tackle count starts again at zero. If the team is tackled on the last tackle, it automatically turns the ball over and the defending team is also awarded the value of a try. Other rules related to kicking, scoring, and restarts are per the rules of the international game.

COACHING POINTS

- Defenders must communicate well and work as a unit to put pressure on the kicker.
- Defenders must retreat well and get behind the ball to return it from their own 20- or 22-metre line or set up a kick, or both.
- Attacking players must choose the correct support options and set up a good kick chase.

VARIATION

If a team kicks the ball into touch as per the rules of the game (i.e., on the full or with a bounce from inside the 22-metre line and on the bounce from outside the 22-metre line), the team is awarded possession and play is restarted by the team that is awarded possession, passing the ball in field from where the ball crossed the touch line, as if taking a quick lineout.

GOAL LINE D

AGES: 14+

Skill execution: 3 ● **Decision making: 3** ● **Speed: 1**

Agility: 3 ● **Endurance: 4** ● **Speed endurance: 2**

OBJECTIVE
To improve goal line defence which is particularly appropriate to the seven-a-side version of rugby.

EQUIPMENT
One ball, eight cones

SET-UP
Mark out a 15-by-30-metre to 20-by-50-metre grid with cones, depending on the age and skill level of your players. Mark 2-metre and 5-metre lines on the grid using cones. Split 14 to 20 players into two teams so that the attacking team has two more players than the defending team. The attacking team starts outside the 5-metre line. The defenders start inside the 2-metre line.

HOW TO PLAY
To begin, the defending team kicks the ball to the attacking team. The defenders may not move out past the 2-metre line. To score, the attacking team must run across the 2-metre line; they do not have to ground the ball. If an attacker is tagged with a two-handed touch, the ball is passed back to the 5-metre line to start the next attack. If the ball is dropped, knocked on, or passed forward, the attack is finished, and the ball is returned to the 5-metre line to start again. The attacking team has two or three minutes to score as many points as possible.

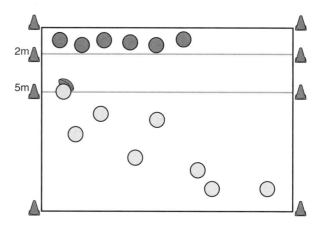

COACHING POINTS
- Defenders must communicate well and work as a unit.
- Attacking players must choose the correct support options.
- Ball carriers must fix or drag defenders.

VARIATIONS
Require the defenders to go onto their chests after making a touch; require the attackers to score by running across the goal line, and if the ball carrier is touched between the goal line and the 2-metre line, the defenders must retreat to the back line and the ball carrier plays the ball from the point of contact.

LINE DEFENCE

AGES: 12+

Skill execution: 3 • Decision making: 3 • Speed: 2

Agility: 2 • Endurance: 4 • Speed endurance: 2

OBJECTIVE
To improve the defence of one's own line while under pressure.

EQUIPMENT
One ball, four cones

SET-UP
Mark out a 15-by-30-metre to 20-by-50-metre grid with cones, depending on the age and skill level of your players. Split 14 to 20 players into two teams so that the attacking team has two more players than the defending team. The attackers start in the field of play at least 5 metres from the goal line ready to receive a kick. The defenders line up on the goal line with the ball.

HOW TO PLAY
To begin, the defending team kicks the ball to the attacking team. If a defender tags the ball carrier with a two-handed touch, the ball carrier goes to ground, and the game is restarted with a play or presentation (this will normally be on a count of three or four). All the defenders, except the markers, or guards, retreat to the goal line. Anytime the ball is dropped, knocked on, or passed forward, the attack is finished, and the game is started again with the defenders kicking the ball out. The game is played for a specific period of time or number of tackles.

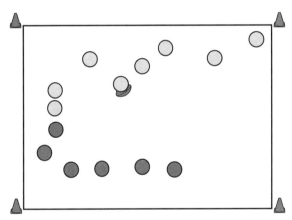

COACHING POINTS
- Defenders must communicate well and work as a unit.
- Attacking players must choose the correct support options.
- Ball carriers must fix or drag defenders.

VARIATIONS
Require the markers, or guards, go to ground; increase the speed of the play or presentation.

PLAYMAKER ATTACK

AGES: 12+

Skill execution: 3 • Decision making: 3 • Speed: 2

Agility: 2 • Endurance: 4 • Speed endurance: 2

OBJECTIVES

For playmakers to develop the ability to organise their team after a turnover in possession, to fix or drag a defender, and to make quick decisions and accurate passes; to learn how to work off the ball, identify space, and run the correct lines; for defenders to practise working as a unit and communicating while fatigued.

EQUIPMENT

One ball, four cones

SET-UP

Mark out a 30-by-40-metre to 40-by-50-metre grid with cones, depending on the age and skill level of your players. Split 14 to 20 players into two teams so that the attacking team has one, two, or three more players than the defending team. The additional player(s), the two lined players in the figure, act as playmakers who always attack (these players will tend to be the 9, 10, and 12 in rugby union and the 9, 6, and 7 in rugby league). The attackers start in the field of play at least 5 metres from the goal line ready to receive a kick. The defenders line up on the goal line with the ball.

HOW TO PLAY

To begin, the attackers receive the ball from you or from the defenders via a drop kick. When a player is touched, the defenders retreat a required distance, and the attackers restart with the touched player presenting or playing the ball. When an infringement occurs, the attacking team turns the ball over, and the playmaker(s) immediately turns around and joins the other team. The attacking team has between four and unlimited tackles with the ball (your choice). The game lasts for a specified period of time, usually two to five minutes.

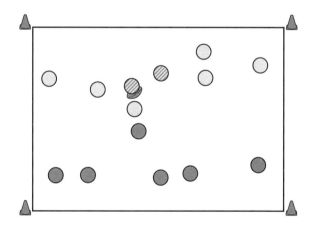

COACHING POINTS

- Playmakers must react quickly on a turnover and organise their attacking team to exploit the situation.
- Teams must react quickly when switching from defence to attack and vice versa.

VARIATION

Introduce a forward pass option in which the attacking team is allowed one forward pass but the team must turn over possession when a player is touched.

TURNOVER GAME

AGES: 11+

Skill execution: 4 ● Decision making: 2 ● Speed: 1

Agility: 2 ● Endurance: 3 ● Speed endurance: 2

OBJECTIVES

To become aware of less-than-optimal skill execution; to learn how to achieve accuracy when executing core skills.

EQUIPMENT

One ball, four cones

SET-UP

The game is played across half a pitch. Split 16 to 20 players into two equal teams. The attackers start in the field of play at least 5 metres from the goal line ready to receive a kick. The defenders line up on the goal line with the ball.

HOW TO PLAY

To begin, the attackers receive the ball from you or from the defenders via a drop kick. When a player is touched, the defenders retreat the required distance, and the attackers restart with the touched player playing the ball with his foot (to himself or to another team member via a play-the-ball or by making the ball available). When a skill infringement occurs (e.g., a poor pass or ball carry), the attacking player puts the ball on the floor, and the other team takes over possession. If a player scores, all attacking players must get behind the goal line before the team turns and attacks the other way. The attacking team has unlimited tackles with the ball. The game lasts for a specified period of time, usually two to five minutes.

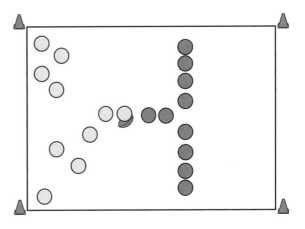

COACHING POINTS

- Attacking players must strive to make accurate passes.
- Ball carriers must run with the ball in two hands.
- Players receiving the ball should have their hands ready with fingers spread.

VARIATIONS

When poor skills are exhibited (e.g., lack of a support runner, a poor play-the-ball or ball presentation), require a turnover; require the guards, or markers, to go to their chests at the breakdown; require tackled players to go to their chests, then their backs, and then their chests (not a roll); require all defenders and attackers to go to their chests.

OPTION GAME

AGES: 14+

Skill execution: 3 • Decision making: 4 • Speed: 2

Agility: 2 • Endurance: 3 • Speed endurance: 2

OBJECTIVES

To learn how to make quick decisions using various passing options; to learn how to work off the ball and identify space.

EQUIPMENT

One ball, four cones

SET-UP

Mark out a 40-by-40-metre to 70-by-70-metre grid with cones, depending on the age and skill level of your players. Split 18 to 24 players into two equal teams. The attackers start in the field of play at least 5 metres from the goal line ready to receive a kick. The defenders line up on the goal line with the ball.

HOW TO PLAY

To begin, the attackers receive the ball from you or from the defenders via a drop kick. When a player is touched, the attacking team restarts play, and the touched player goes onto his chest, rolls onto his back, and goes back the other way onto his chest before playing the ball. The game is two-handed touch (between the thigh and chest), and kicking is not allowed. The team in possession has unlimited tackles with the ball. There must be an option runner in each play; otherwise, the attacking team must turn the ball over (when there is a turnover, the new team in possession always attacks the long end). The option runner must be in a good position to take a pass from the ball carrier, but may end up acting as a decoy. After a score, the attacking team restarts with a play-the-ball 5 metres out from the try line attacking the other end. All players must be onside at this point; otherwise, the team turns over possession.

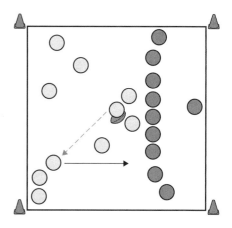

COACHING POINTS

- Ball carriers and option runners must run effective lines that attract defenders and create space.
- Players must work hard off the ball to offer themselves as option runners

VARIATION

Introduce a forward pass option in which the attacking team is allowed one forward pass but the team must turn over possession when a player is touched.

SHAPE GAME

AGES: 15+

Skill execution: 3 ● Decision making: 4 ● Speed: 2

Agility: 2 ● Endurance: 3 ● Speed endurance: 2

OBJECTIVES

To learn how to develop attacking shape around the breakdown to create passing options; to learn how to work off the ball and identify space.

EQUIPMENT

One ball, four cones

SET-UP

Mark out a 40-by-40-metre to 60-by-70-metre grid with cones. The attackers start in the field of play at least 5 metres from the goal line ready to receive a kick. The defenders line up on the goal line with the ball.

HOW TO PLAY

To begin, the attackers receive the ball from you or from the defenders via a drop kick. The game is played with unlimited tackles over a set time period (e.g., three minutes). The attacking team must establish its attacking shape around the breakdown with ball players, support runners, option runners, and decoy runners in place. You control the minimum time of the breakdown (e.g., four seconds). Penalties can be imposed on the team for not setting its shape (e.g., they must hand the ball over or restart that particular attack). Fewer players can be used for this game, in which case teams should turn the ball over for each infringement; this is because a smaller version focuses on improving individual players'

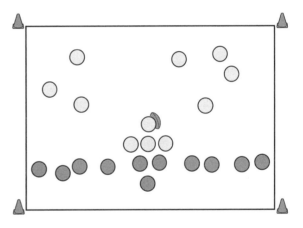

understanding. With a larger number of players, the focus is on team play and presumes that individual players already have efficient core skills and an understanding of shape and their role within it; therefore, there should be no need to turn the ball over for minor skill infringements.

COACHING POINTS

- Players must get into the attacking shape by offering themselves as ball carriers, decoys, or supporting runners.
- Playmakers must communicate and organise the attacking players well.
- Playmakers must take the team up the field in an organised manner but be ready to exploit any advantages and weaknesses in the defensive team that may occur.

VARIATION

Require your team to play specific shapes based on the style of play of the team they are playing against next in the season.

TRIPLE OVERLOAD TOUCH

AGES: ALL

Skill execution: 3 ● Decision making: 3 ● Speed: 3

Agility: 2 ● Endurance: 4 ● Speed endurance: 2

OBJECTIVES

To learn how to fix or drag a defender and make quick decisions and accurate passes; to learn how to work off the ball, identify space, and run the correct lines; for defenders to practise working as a unit and communicating when fatigued.

EQUIPMENT

One ball, four cones

SET-UP

Mark out a 30-by-40-metre to 50-by-60-metre grid with cones, depending on the age and skill level of your players. Split up to 18 players into two equal teams. When using 18 players, nine attackers position near their goal line and three defenders position 5 metres back from the attackers. The remaining six defenders (two groups of three) position outside the grid along the sideline (with fewer players, use the same principles of dividing the defensive team into three subunits).

HOW TO PLAY

To begin, the attacking team receives the ball from you or from the defenders via a drop kick from the goal line. When a player is touched, the defenders retreat a required distance, and the attackers restart with the touched player playing the ball with her or his foot or presenting the ball (your choice). The attacking team is allowed six tackles with the ball. At the end of each series of tackles, whether a score occurs or not, the attackers sprint back behind the start line and immediately collect the ball to attack (all attackers must get behind this line before the ball can be played). The attacking team has the ball for a set number of tackles or a specified period of time, usually one or two minutes, against each number of defenders. When the time is over or the tackle count reached, three more defenders are added (i.e., 9v6); the game continues until the final three defenders are added.

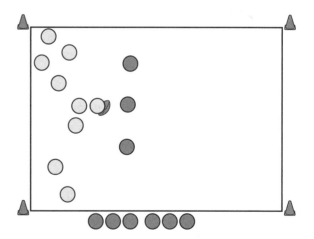

COACHING POINTS

- Ball carriers must engage defenders.
- Attacking players must be accurate and not get over-excited when playing against the limited number of defenders.

VARIATIONS

Use a descending number of defenders (i.e., 9v9, 9v6, 9v3); allow the attacking team two tackles against three defenders, four tackles against six defenders, and six tackles against nine defenders.

BASE CONE TOUCH

AGES: ALL

Skill execution: 3 • Decision making: 3 • Speed: 3

Agility: 2 • Endurance: 4 • Speed endurance: 3

OBJECTIVES

To learn how to fix or drag a defender and make quick decisions and accurate passes; to learn how to work off the ball, identify space, and run the correct lines; for attacking players to learn how to support the break and make correct decisions; for defenders to practise working as a unit and communicating when fatigued.

EQUIPMENT

At least 10 balls, six cones

SET-UP

Mark out a 50-by-70-metre grid with cones. Split 16 to 24 players into two equal teams. The attackers start within the field of play at least 5 metres from the goal line ready to receive a kick. The defenders line up on the goal line with the ball.

HOW TO PLAY

To begin, the attacking team receives the ball from you or from the defenders via a drop kick. A defender who has touched a player must retreat behind his own line and around the centre cone, while the rest of the defenders line up 3 to 7 metres back from the tackled player. The attackers restart with the touched player playing the ball with his foot. The attacking team has unlimited tackles with the ball. When an infringement occurs, the attackers sprint back behind the start line and immediately collect another ball to attack (all attackers must get behind this line before the ball can be played). If a player scores, all attacking players must get behind the goal line before the team turns and attacks the other way. Each team has the ball for a specified period of time, usually two to five minutes.

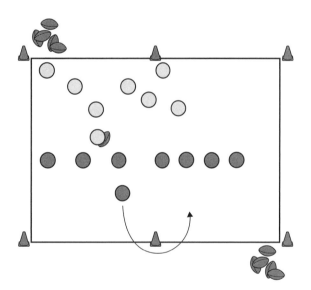

COACHING POINTS

- Ball carriers must have good vision to be able commit defenders and pass to players in space.
- Support runners must choose their running lines well.
- Attacking players must execute 2v1 situations efficiently, especially when faced with players returning from the cone.

VARIATIONS

Add cones to the sidelines and require players to go around a sideline cone after a touch; require two touches before a player retreats to the cone; require the guards, or markers, to go to their chests at the breakdown; require tackled players to go to their chests or to go onto their chests, then their backs, and then their chests (not a roll); rather than playing for a specific time with the ball, the attacking team holds the ball for a specific number of tackles and turns the ball over on an infringement.

FAST BALL

AGES: 14+

Skill execution: 3 • Decision making: 3 • Speed: 2

Agility: 2 • Endurance: 3 • Speed endurance: 2

OBJECTIVES

To practise accurate passing from the breakdown in rugby union, develop a fast attacking game with support runners, and practise getting to the breakdown quickly.

EQUIPMENT

One ball, tackle shields, four cones

SET-UP

The game is played on a full pitch or between the 5-metre lines. Split 22 players into two equal teams. The attacking team positions near its goal line. The defending team positions at the halfway line; up to half the defenders hold tackle shields.

HOW TO PLAY

To begin, the defending team kicks the ball to the attackers from the halfway line. The game is two-handed touch. Attacking players who are touched go to ground and present the ball; as they are touched, you call, '1, 2, 3, away.' If the attacking team does not get the ball away in this time, it forfeits possession. Ball carriers who hit shield holders must turn and make the ball available to another player who has latched on before the ball is available. The attacking team has the ball for an unlimited number of tackles unless it forfeits possession.

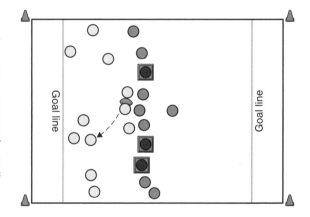

COACHING POINTS

- Tackled players must present the ball well in the tackle.
- Players need to pass accurately from the breakdown.
- Players need to work hard off the ball to get into good support positions.

VARIATIONS

Introduce another ball to another part of the field and allow either side to gain possession; the attacking team loses possession if it does not clear threats near the maul or establish attacking pillars at the ruck; the defensive team is penalised yardage if it does not commit the correct numbers to the breakdown.

THREE SWEEPERS

AGES: 12+

Skill execution: 3 • Decision making: 3 • Speed: 4

Agility: 2 • Endurance: 3 • Speed endurance: 2

OBJECTIVES

For attackers to practise exploiting large blind, or short, sides and to exploit an overload of numbers; to develop good decision-making skills after a line break.

EQUIPMENT

One ball, eight cones

SET-UP

The game is played lengthways either on a full- or three-quarter-length pitch; the width is full size with two 10- to 15-metre outside zones. Mark the grid with cones and the outside zones with cones. Split 20 players into two equal teams. The attacking team positions along its goal line with the ball. Seven defenders position 5 to 10 metres back in the centre zone; two wingers position in the outside zones 10 metres behind the seven defenders. One fullback positions in the centre zone 10 metres behind the seven defenders.

HOW TO PLAY

Normal touch rules apply. The attacking team has four or six tackles in which to score. The defending wingers must stay in the outside zone and 10 metres behind the rest of the defensive line, and the fullback must stay 10 metres behind the line but in the centre zone. The winger may move forward only when an attacking ball carrier enters the outside zone. Other defenders may enter this zone only when the ball has been passed into it or the ball carrier has entered this zone. Decide whether to allow the attacking team to use kicks.

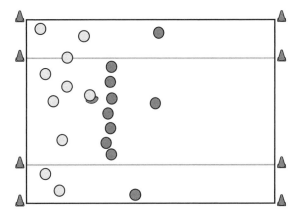

COACHING POINTS

- Ball carriers must fix the winger and covering defenders to create space in the outside zone.
- Ball carriers must draw and pass and not run across the field allowing the cover to push them to the touch line.

VARIATION

Allow two touches to be used in the sweeper zone (i.e., the attacking player can pass after being touched by a defender), and require that the attacking team turn the ball over if an attacking player is touched for a second time before having an opportunity to pass the ball to a support runner.

ZONE TOUCH

AGES: ALL

Skill execution: 3 ● Decision making: 3 ● Speed: 2

Agility: 2 ● Endurance: 4 ● Speed endurance: 3

OBJECTIVES

To learn how to fix or drag a defender and make quick decisions and accurate passes; to learn how to work off the ball, identify space, and run the correct lines; for attacking players to learn how to support the break; for defenders to learn how to fill in around the breakdown.

EQUIPMENT

One ball, eight cones

SET-UP

The game is played lengthways on a full pitch. The pitch is divided into three zones of equal width which are marked with cones. Split 18 players into two teams with 12 players on the attacking team and 6 players on the defending team (with fewer players, maintain a two-to-one ratio). The defending team positions at the halfway line, and the attacking team is spread out in the field of play in front of its goal line.

HOW TO PLAY

Normal touch rules apply. All the defenders must be in the zone where the tackle takes place; any player not in the zone is offside, and sanctions are applied. Kicking is not allowed. The attacking team has six (or unlimited) tackles in which to score. If the team scores, play restarts 5 metres from the goal line opposite where the try was scored (i.e., not in the middle of the field). All players must be onside before the ball can be played. If they infringe with the ball or fail to score, they sprint back and restart 5 metres from their own goal line, and all players must be behind the ball. The attacking team has the ball for specified period of time, usually four minutes.

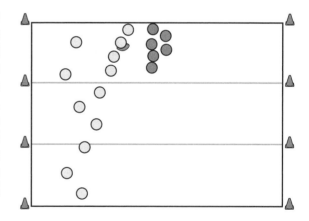

COACHING POINTS

- The attacking team must hold defenders and pass the ball.
- Support players must run good lines to hold defenders.
- Ball carriers must choose between short and long passes.

VARIATIONS

Adjust the speed of the breakdown; use equal numbers of defenders and attackers and divide the defensive team into three groups (right, left, and middle), and require them to stay in their respective zones throughout the game to encourage the attackers to flood zones with a large number of players to create an attacking overload.

TWO-BALL TOUCH

AGES: 15+

Skill execution: 3 ● Decision making: 3 ● Speed: 3

Agility: 2 ● Endurance: 3 ● Speed endurance: 3

OBJECTIVE

To develop the ability to react to a loose ball or turnover on both attack and defence.

EQUIPMENT

Two balls, four cones

SET-UP

Mark out a 40-by-50-metre to 60-by-75-metre grid with cones, depending on the age and skill level of your players. Split 14 to 22 players into two equal teams. The defending team positions along the centre of the grid, and the attacking team positions in the field of play in front of its goal line.

HOW TO PLAY

To begin, the defending team kicks the ball to the attacking team. Kicking is not allowed in general play. The attacking team has unlimited tackles in which to score. After scoring, the team restarts play by kicking the ball back into the field of play to the other team from behind the goal line. If the team infringes with the ball, you immediately throw a second ball behind the defending team to collect. During general play, you can blow your whistle and throw or kick a second ball to another area of the field for either team to react to and collect. The game lasts for a specific period of time, usually 5 to 10 minutes.

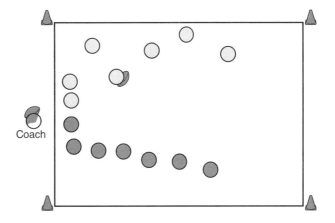

COACHING POINTS

- Players must react appropriately to the second ball.
- Attacking players must get behind the ball in an onside position.
- Defending players must rapidly reorganise and realign their defence.

VARIATION

Adjust the speed of the breakdown.

OFFLOAD TOUCH

AGES: 14+

Skill execution: 3 ● Decision making: 4 ● Speed: 2

Agility: 2 ● Endurance: 4 ● Speed endurance: 2

OBJECTIVES

To develop the ability to fix a defender and make quick decisions and accurate passes; to learn how to work off the ball, identify space, and run the correct lines; for defenders to practise nominating and defending particular spaces.

EQUIPMENT

At least eight balls, four cones

SET-UP

Mark out a 40-by-50-metre to 60-by-75-metre grid with cones, depending on the age and skill level of your players. Split 15 to 23 players into two teams, giving the attacking team an extra player (if you have an even number of players, give the attacking team two extra players). The defending team positions along the centre of the grid, and the attacking team positions in the field of play in front of its goal line.

HOW TO PLAY

To begin, the defending team kicks the ball to the attacking team. Kicking is not allowed in general play. The attacking team has four, six, or unlimited tackles in which to score. When players are first touched, they have the option of passing the ball or going on one knee before playing or presenting the ball; on the second touch, they must go to one knee and play or present the ball. Focusing on good decision making and good support play, the attacking team aims to keep the ball alive and pull defenders out of the line. If it scores, play restarts by the defending team kicking the ball back into the field of play from behind the goal line. If the attacking team infringes with the ball in the unlimited tackle variation, the players immediately sprint back and collect another ball from behind their line. In the limited tackle version, in the case of an infringement, the defending team receives

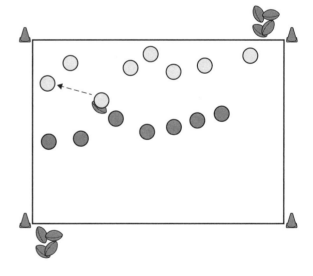

possession, and one or two players from the original attacking team join to create an overload of numbers. The game lasts for a specific period of time, usually 5 to 10 minutes.

COACHING POINTS

- Players should pass the ball to support runners to keep the ball alive.
- Ball carriers must make correct decisions and choose appropriate passing options.
- Support runners must work off the ball to make themselves available and run into gaps.

VARIATIONS

Require a touched player to pass the ball to a support runner or turn the ball over, and support players who are touched must play the ball or restart the game in the agreed manner; require every ball carrier to pass the ball to a support runner before being touched twice, otherwise that player's team turns the ball over; divide the pitch into three equal zones as in Zone Touch on page 142, and designate zones in which normal touch rules apply and zones in which two-touch rules apply; allow kicking; require players to do a press-up after passing the ball; have some defenders (e.g., 3 or 4) defend behind the line as sweepers to create space for the offload to exploit.

SHIELD OFFLOAD OPTION

AGES: 14+

Skill execution: 3 • Decision making: 4 • Speed: 2

Agility: 2 • Endurance: 3 • Speed endurance: 2

OBJECTIVE

To learn how to make appropriate decisions around the offload, such as the proper depth and timing of runs.

EQUIPMENT

One ball, 8 to 10 shields of two different colours, four cones

SET-UP

Mark out a 40-by-40-metre to 60-by-60-metre grid with cones, depending on the age and skill level of your players. Split 16 to 20 players into two equal teams. Each of the players on the defending team holds a tackle shield. The defending team positions along the centre of the grid, and the attacking team positions near its goal line with the ball.

HOW TO PLAY

To begin, the defending team kicks the ball to the attacking team. Kicking is not allowed in general play. After catching the kick-off, the attacking players run towards the shield holders with the ball (the attacking players do not bust through the shields). Attacking players who make contact with a shield of one colour must to ground and present the ball, or play the ball; when they make contact with a shield of the other colour, they must offload the ball in front of the line to a support runner. The attacking team has the ball for a set period of time (e.g., three minutes). If the attacking team scores, all the players must cross the goal line before the team realigns 5 to 10 metres out and attacks the other way. If the team infringes, either the ball is turned over or the entire team must sprint back behind its own goal line and start again on its own 5- or 10-metre line.

COACHING POINTS

- Attackers must learn to support the ball carriers and react to the offload.
- Players should not wait for the next play.

VARIATION

On hitting a shield, the ball carrier carries on going forward and passes the ball in or through the defensive line to a support runner. In this case there must be at least two defenders without shields acting as sweepers behind the defensive line; have some players without shields to effect a tackle.

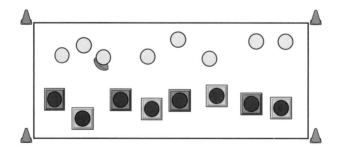

SPOT GAME

AGES: 14+

Skill execution: 3 ● **Decision making: 4** ● **Speed: 2**

Agility: 2 ● **Endurance: 3** ● **Speed endurance: 2**

OBJECTIVES

To develop decision-making skills around the offload such as depth and timing runs; to develop the ability to move the ball to areas of the field where weak defenders (spots) have been identified.

EQUIPMENT

One ball, four cones

SET-UP

Mark out a 40-by-40-metre to 60-by-60-metre grid with cones, depending on the age and skill level of your players. Split 16 to 20 players into two equal teams. The defending team positions along the centre of the grid, and the attacking team positions in the field of play near its goal line. Two defenders are identified as spot players, the two lined players in the figure.

HOW TO PLAY

To begin, the defending team kicks the ball to the attacking team. Normal touch rules apply except when the ball carrier takes the ball into a spot, in which case any of the following can happen:

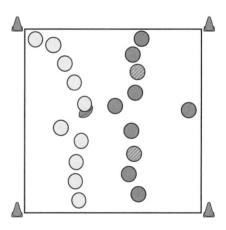

- For a league team, the spot could represent a fast play-the-ball, whereas being touched by a non-spot would result in the ball being started with a slow play-the-ball. In union, the bibbed players could represent front row players caught defending wide from a line-out.
- The attacking team could score points every time it hits into the spot.
- The ball carrier of the attacking team could break through the spot and bust the line.
- The attacking team could offload the ball where the ball carrier is touched by the spot.

The attacking team has the ball for a set period of time (e.g., three minutes). If the attacking team scores, all the players must cross the goal line before the team realigns 5 or 10 metres out and attacks the other way. If the team infringes, either the ball is turned over or the entire team must sprint back behind its own goal line and start again on its own 5- or 10-metre line.

COACHING POINTS

- Playmakers, or halfbacks, on the attacking team must learn to move the team into key areas to attack the spots.
- Ball carriers and support runners must make correct decisions around the spots.
- The defending team must not be allowed to hide its spots behind other players.

VARIATION

If the attacking team is allowed to bust, there must be a fullback in place, in which case the attackers must flood through. If the ball carrier is tackled without support, the team may be penalised with a turnover of possession, a loss of yardage, or having to return to the start line.

DEFENSIVE RUCK GAME

AGES: 12+

Skill execution: 1 ● Decision making: 1 ● Speed: 2

Agility: 2 ● Endurance: 4 ● Speed endurance: 3

OBJECTIVES
To learn how to organise the defence around the play-the-ball or ruck area; to improve defensive communication.

EQUIPMENT
One ball, four cones

SET-UP
Mark a 30-by-40-metre to 40-by-70-metre grid with cones. Split 16 to 20 players into two equal teams. The attackers position 5 metres from their goal line with the ball. The defenders position 5 to 10 metres back.

HOW TO PLAY
To begin, the ball carrier taps the ball and runs forward or passes the ball to another player. In league play, when the attacking player is touched, the markers get set in the correct place. The other defenders retreat the required distance, tie in to the required width from the tackle, and number off to ensure that the attackers do not have extra players at one side of the tackle. The first defender from the tackle may call 'A,' and the second may call 'B.' When touched, attacking players go onto their chests, then their backs, and over to their chests (not a roll) before playing the ball. If you blow your whistle on the touch, the attacker drops to her or his chest and executes a quick play-the-ball. The attacking team has the ball for a large number of tackles (e.g., 18) or for a specific period of time unless it loses possession.

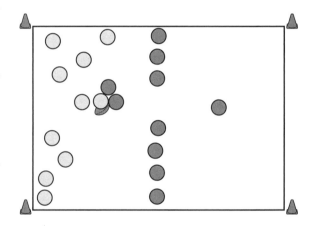

In union play, the attacking team starts with the ball carrier lying down and making the ball available. When the attacking player is touched, the two nearest defenders go to their chests, and the other defenders retreat the required distance, number off, and nominate the guards and bodyguards. When touched, the attacking player goes to ground and makes the ball available, and the two nearest attackers mark the defenders who are on their chests. If you blow your whistle on the touch, the attacker immediately turns and gives the ball to a scrum half, who chooses to either run (snipe) or pass the ball away from the breakdown. The attacking team has the ball for a large number of tackles (e.g., 18) or for a specific period of time unless it loses possession.

COACHING POINTS
- Defenders should use the calls and language that their team uses on match days to designate their positions.
- You can allow varying levels of contact up to full contact.

VARIATIONS
Allow the attacking team to gain extra tackles if the defenders exhibit poor organisation (e.g., fail to number off or are left on the ground); in the union version, the two attacking players can step over the tackled player or clear the threats (i.e., the nearest defenders to the breakdown), which will vary depending on whether touch rules or contact rules are being followed; guards, or markers, must go to their chests at the breakdown; all defenders or attackers must go to their chests as each tackle is made to create an extreme conditioning element.

DOMINANT TACKLE

AGES: 13+

Skill execution: 2 ● Decision making: 2 ● Speed: 2

Agility: 2 ● Endurance: 3 ● Speed endurance: 2

OBJECTIVE

For rugby league players to learn how to dominate the tackle area and control the speed of the opponent's play-the-ball.

EQUIPMENT

One ball, four cones

SET-UP

Mark out a 30-by-40-metre to 50-by-70-metre grid with cones, depending on the age and skill level of your players. Split 16 to 22 players into two equal teams (or slightly overload the defence). The attacking team positions 5 metres from its goal line with the ball. The defenders position 5 to 7 metres back from the attackers.

HOW TO PLAY

To begin, the ball carrier taps the ball and runs forward or passes the ball to another player. When the attacking player is tackled, the defenders must lock off the ball and aim to put the player on his or her back (or at least control the player on the floor). The defenders must then unload correctly and get into the marker position. The game is played for six tackles; however, the tackle count is restarted under the following conditions:

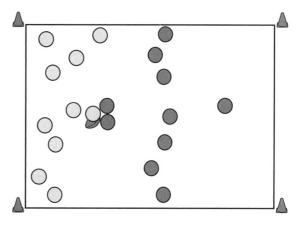

- The attacking team plays the ball while one of the defenders is on the floor.
- The dummy half scoots and is not tackled by a marker.
- The ball carrier offloads in the tackle when two or more tacklers are in contact.

The attacking team loses a tackle if the defenders are completely dominant when putting the player on his or her back. The defenders must unload correctly by getting off the tackled player in the order that is most effective at slowing down the play-the-ball.

COACHING POINTS

- Defenders must communicate about who is in the tackle and who has the ball.
- Tacklers must keep their heads up and make first contact with their shoulders.
- Tacklers must ensure that the ball carrier does not pass the ball in the tackle.
- Defenders must control the tackled player and put him onto his back.
- The tackler who has locked the ball and is on top of the chest of the player will allow the other tackler to leave and assume the marker position before he or she gets up and assumes the other marker position. There should always be two or more tacklers involved.

VARIATION

Require specific types of tackles or two- or three-player tackles.

OUT TO IN, IN TO OUT

AGES: 12+

Skill execution: 3 ● Decision making: 3 ● Speed: 2

Agility: 2 ● Endurance: 3 ● Speed endurance: 2

OBJECTIVE

For defenders to develop the ability to use various defensive patterns according to the situations they are facing.

EQUIPMENT

One ball, four cones

SET-UP

Mark out a 40-by-50-metre to 50-by-60-metre grid with cones, depending on the age and skill level of your players. Split 16 players into two teams (10 defenders and 6 attackers). The attacking team positions in the field of play. The defending team positions along the centre of the grid.

HOW TO PLAY

To begin, the defending team kicks the ball to the attacking team. When a player is touched, the defenders retreat a required distance, and the attackers restart with the touched player playing or presenting the ball. When an infringement occurs, the attackers get behind the start line and are given another ball to attack (all attackers must get behind this line before the ball can be played). If a player scores, all attacking players must get behind the goal line before the team turns and attacks the other way. The attacking team has 4, 6, or unlimited tackles with the ball. After each phase, the number of players changes in this manner: 7 attackers against 9 defenders, 8 attackers against 8 defenders, 9 attackers against 7 defenders, 10 attackers against 6 defenders. In other words, ensure that the attackers gain a player and the defenders lose a player. Each phase of the game lasts for the required time (normally two to three minutes).

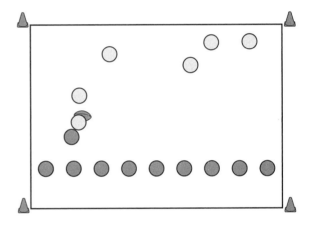

COACHING POINTS

- Do not tell the defenders how to defend.
- With a large defensive overload, the defenders should defend up and in.
- When the numbers are equal, the defensive strategy will depend on the position of the ball in relation to the width of the pitch and to the number of players at, near, and at either side of the breakdown.
- With a large offensive overload, the defenders will defend up and out, but may on occasion fly up to cut off an attack at the source.
- Players must communicate as a unit.

PRE-EXHAUST THE DEFENCE

AGES: 15+

Skill execution: 2 ● Decision making: 3 ● Speed: 2

Agility: 3 ● Endurance: 5 ● Speed endurance: 3

OBJECTIVE

To learn how to make key defensive decisions while fatigued.

EQUIPMENT

At least five balls, four cones, tackle bags

SET-UP

Mark out a 30-by-30-metre to 40-by-60-metre grid with cones, depending on the age and skill level of your players. Split 18 to 30 players into three equal groups. Group 1 holds tackle bags 5 to 10 metre behind the goal line. Group 2 lines up opposite the bags facing away from the pitch. Group 3 spreads out in the field ready to attack the goal line.

HOW TO PLAY

On your command, group 2 makes a predetermined number of tackles on the bags that group 1 is holding. After making the tackles on the bags, group 2 turns, enters the grid, and kicks a ball to group 3, which immediately attacks for six tackles. Normal touch rules apply. If group 3 scores within its set of six tackles, it gets one more set in which to score. If group 3 makes an error within the set, it forfeits possession, and group 2 becomes the attackers, group 3 holds the bags, and group 1 becomes the defenders.

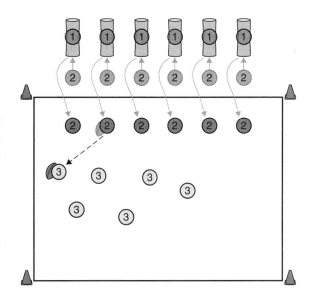

COACHING POINTS

- Players should strive to maintain unity of defence when tired.
- Players must communicate effectively as a unit.

VARIATION

Remove players from the defensive line after each tackle to increase pressure on the defence.

ONE-TEAM KICK

AGES: 13+

Skill execution: 3 • Decision making: 3 • Speed: 3

Agility: 2 • Endurance: 3 • Speed endurance: 2

OBJECTIVE
To develop the ability to execute a kicking strategy and maintain possession as a team.

EQUIPMENT
One ball, four cones

SET-UP
Mark out a 50-by-70-metre grid with cones. Split 14 to 20 players into two teams. The defending team positions along the centre of the grid, and the attacking team positions in the field of play near its goal line.

HOW TO PLAY
To begin, the defending team kicks the ball to the attacking team. When an attacking player is touched, the defender stays as a marker and the attackers restart with the touched player playing the ball with her or his foot. The attacking team has four tackles with the ball. On the fourth tackle, the attacking team must score or execute a kick. When the defending team receives the ball, it has four tackles in which to score, but is not allowed a kicking option. In the second attacking phase, the same rules apply, but the teams are allowed five tackles, and in the third set, six tackles. If either team infringes, the ball is turned over. If the kicking team does not score or get the ball away on the last play, it is classed as an infringement. When the sequence is complete, play switches, and the other team has the four, five, and six kicking options.

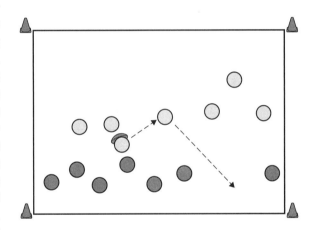

COACHING POINTS
- The kicking team must set up its kick well and choose good kicking options with an effective chase.
- The non-kicking team must put pressure on the kicker and also defend well in the early tackles to cut the attacking team's yardage down.

VARIATIONS
Require the guards, or markers, to go to their chests at the breakdown; require tackled players to go to their chests or to go onto their chests, then their backs, and then their chest (not a roll); require all defenders to go onto their chests; adjust the number of tackles prior to a kick; allow one team six tackles but no kick while the other team has only three possessions but is allowed to kick.

KICK RETURN

AGES: 15+

Skill execution: 3 ● Decision making: 3 ● Speed: 3

Agility: 2 ● Endurance: 3 ● Speed endurance: 4

OBJECTIVES

To develop kick chase organisation and the counterattacking skills of the kick reception team.

EQUIPMENT

One ball, four cones

SET-UP

The game is played on a 45-by-50-metre to 70-by-100-metre pitch marked with cones. Split 16 to 22 players into two teams. The attacking team positions about 20 metres from its goal line. The defending team position 7 to 10 metres back, and three of the players act as the back three (i.e., full back and two wingers), positioning 10 to 20 metres behind the other defenders.

HOW TO PLAY

To begin, the attacking team kicks the ball after a pass or play-the-ball to the kicker. The kicker kicks the ball to the defending team's back three, who then return the ball and are tackled. The defending team has another play in which to set up its kick. If the ball bounces out of touch, the non-kicking team starts with a breakdown adjacent to where the ball crossed the sideline. If the ball goes out of bounds without bouncing, the team restarts from where the kick was made. A team can score a try from an attacking kick or from a skilful counterattack. All infringements while in possession are penalised by a turnover.

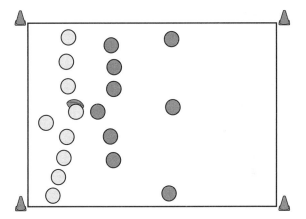

COACHING POINTS

- Players should use good kick chase organisation.
- The back three players should use counterattacking options.

VARIATIONS

Allow one team two tackles and the other team six tackles in which to score or set up its kick; award points for a good kick chase causing the back three catching the ball to be tackled within a set distance (e.g., 10 or 20 metres of the goal line).

LINEOUT

AGES: 15+

Skill execution: 3 ● Decision making: 2 ● Speed: 1

Agility: 2 ● Endurance: 1 ● Speed endurance: 1

OBJECTIVES

To develop accurate lineout skills; to practise scrum half passing and fly half kicking.

EQUIPMENT

One ball, four cones

SET-UP

The game is played on a full pitch using 20 players with, ideally, a full pack of forwards, a fly half, and a scrum half.

HOW TO PLAY

To begin, the attacking team has a lineout 10 metres from its line. The lineout can be contested or uncontested (your choice). When a team wins possession, the scrum half or fly half kicks for touch. A successful touch kick results in a lineout with the throw to the kicking team (as the teams become more successful, the throw can be awarded according to the rules of the game). An unsuccessful kick results in the lineout taking place again with the throw awarded to the other team. The team scores with a drop goal by the fly half.

COACHING POINTS

- Players must use good throwing and kicking techniques.
- The attacking team should practise its lineout quickly and under pressure.

VARIATIONS

Allow the teams to score by a catch and driving maul; put a time constraint on each lineout between the time the ball leaves the field and the time of the lineout; add a complete back division, and allow the attacking team the option of attacking after winning a lineout within the opponents' 22-metre zone.

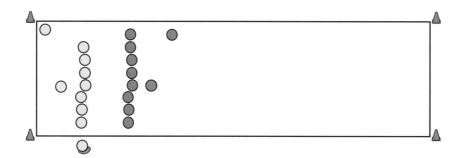

LOCK AND TURN

AGES: 15+

Skill execution: 3 ● Decision making: 3 ● Speed: 2

Agility: 2 ● Endurance: 3 ● Speed endurance: 2

OBJECTIVES

To develop good kick-off, catching, and lifting skills and good transition play.

EQUIPMENT

One ball, four cones

SET-UP

The game is played on a full-sized pitch. Split at least 18 players into equal teams with three pods of three players each on one team and nine players on the other team. Players start on either side of the halfway line and about 5 to 10 metres back, facing each other.

HOW TO PLAY

To begin the game, throw or kick the ball up in the air to the pods, who catch the ball using lifting pod skills. The other team chases and forms a controlled maul. After the maul, one of the teams attacks for a specific number of tackles (normally three). You choose the team in possession and the number of tackles.

COACHING POINTS

- Players must use good lifting and catching techniques.
- Players must be able to turn after catching the ball.
- Non-catchers must ensure correct timing when they lock on to the catcher.

VARIATIONS

Allow the team that has kicked the ball to run and challenge (legally) for possession; a successful catch allows the team six possessions in which to score; an unsuccessful catch allows the non-offending team six possessions in which to score; allow a fully-contested maul.

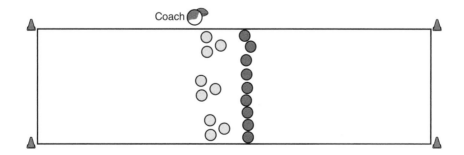

CHAPTER 9

Fitness Requirements for Rugby

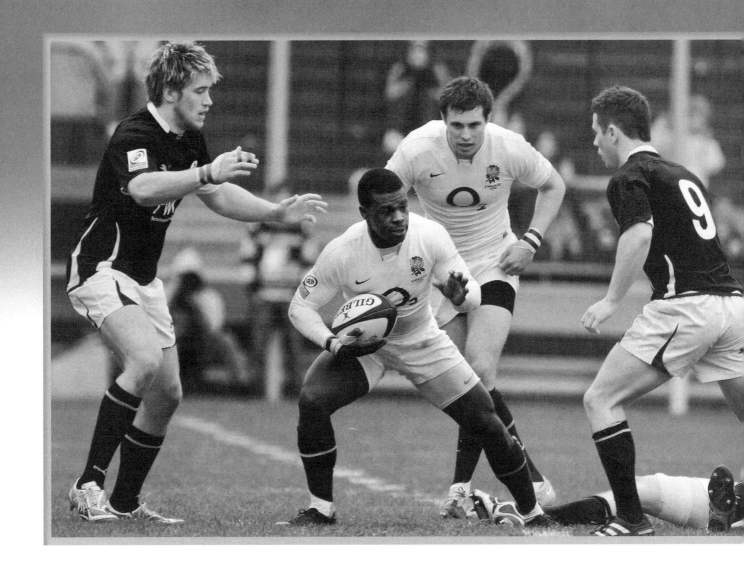

Over the years, rugby coaches have typically used traditional conditioning activities (e.g., running without the ball) to elicit improvements in physical fitness. This form of training, however, challenges only the body's energy systems. Given that most country teams participate in only two 90-minute sessions per week, valuable training time is lost if players spend unnecessarily long periods without the ball in their hands. Clearly, you need to optimise training time to develop as many fitness components as possible, while also providing drills that develop decision-making and problem-solving skills (Gabbett 2001).

If you see your players for only two 90-minute sessions per week, maximise their training by putting them in opposed, gamelike situations for as much of the time as possible. Doing so will not only improve their fitness levels, but also make them better decision makers. Conditioning games elicit an intensity equal or superior to that of traditional conditioning activities and provide considerably greater total work time (Gamble 2004). Players also find them more enjoyable. Skill-based conditioning games are a practical way to develop thinking players, while also promoting skilful performance under pressure and when fatigued (Charlesworth 1999).

One of the key principles of training is specificity, which states that training should be specific to the sport or game that the training is aimed at improving. Athletes in sports such as swimming and cycling do most, if not all, of their training in the mode in which they perform (i.e., swimmers swim and cyclists cycle). They carry out additional strength and conditioning training using weights and other methods.

Support training in rugby includes weight training and speed and agility activities. Players also engage in power endurance training such as strongman training. Individual players sometimes look to improve their aerobic capacity or body composition with non-specific methods such as stationary cycling, rowing, and cross-training. However, most rugby training to improve energy system work capacity should involve running. Running activities should be as specific to the game of rugby as possible, involving the movement patterns and energy systems relevant to the game.

Try to combine skills, game-specific agility, decision-making, and endurance training if at all possible. You can do this by using skill drills along with game-related conditioning activities and games, making sure to plan and monitor the intensity closely. Also, within a field training session you can intersperse these with strength-related activities such as strongman events and wrestling-type activities.

Rugby-Specific Fitness

Both codes of rugby are defined as collision sports (i.e., players purposely collide with each other). Other collision sports are American football, Australian rules football, ice hockey, and Gaelic football. These sports are very different in their rules and, therefore, in their technical and physical demands. Australian football is played on a bigger field than rugby is, and the ball is in play for up to 30 minutes a quarter, resulting in players sometimes running more than 11 kilometres in a match. These players clearly need a high degree of cardiorespiratory fitness.

An American football game consists of four 15-minute quarters (12-minute quarters in high school football, and often shorter at lower levels). Because the game stops after each play, players do not require a high level of cardiorespiratory fitness. Professional (NFL) and college American football players exhibit extremely high levels of strength and power, much higher than those generally seen in rugby players of either code. The reasons for this are the shorter season and hence longer preparation phase, the lack of interference from the aerobic activities needing to be trained in rugby, and the longer strength training history of most players.

Rugby union and rugby league sit between the extremes of Australian and American football. Both codes of rugby involve the ball carrier being stopped and sometimes put to ground by one or more opponents. In rugby league, the tackled player retains the ball; in rugby union, there can be a contest for the ball in either a ruck, in which the tackled player has gone to ground, or a maul, in which the tackled player remains standing. In addition, both sports require speed, agility, a moderately high level of strength and power, and a moderate to high level of cardiorespiratory fitness.

The various components of fitness have a bearing on the outcome of the collision, or tackle. A team that dominates the tackle normally wins the match. Ball carriers need to use good footwork (agility) to try to avoid a collision or to find the opponents' edges and enter collisions on their terms. They need power to break through the initial impact and acceleration to get away if they break the defender.

When the tackle is made, the defending and attacking players need strength to dominate the collision to finish it on their terms. Defenders need leg strength to lift and drive an opponent and also upper-body strength to twist and turn the ball carrier.

The play-the-ball is a key area in rugby league. Ball carriers attempt to land in a prone position to get the ball back into play for their team as quickly as possible. Defenders attempt to turn players onto their backs and facing away from the attacking goal line. Some teams try to hold opponents upright, to keep the ball carrier upright before putting to ground, in order to gain time in this area. All this involves specific technical skills and strength and is also affected by factors such as acceleration and change of direction speed (Gabbett 2009).

Maintaining the efficiency of the tackle also depends on strength endurance and cardiorespiratory endurance. Fatigue results in progressive reductions in tackle technique; studies have shown a significant association between estimated endurance ($\dot{V}O_2$max) and agility and fatigue-induced decrements in tackle technique (Gabbett 2008). The ability to maintain muscular power when experiencing game-specific fatigue appears critical to preventing fatigue-induced decrements in tackling technique.

Gabbett (2005) found that the majority of rugby league injuries occurred in the tackle, suggesting that fitness levels affect the rate of player injuries. In rugby union it was also found the tackle, ruck, and maul elements of match play presented the highest risk of injury for all players' (Brooks, Fuller, Kemp, and Reddin 2005).

In the ruck, which is specific to rugby union, tackled players are off their feet and tackled to ground. To secure possession of the ball for their own team, supporting players must aggressively move opponents away from this area.

Arriving at the ruck first requires tactical understanding, technical skill, and speed. To move opponents once at the ruck, players must have the correct technique, adopt suitable body positions, and have a high degree of power and strength. The average ruck per English premiership match lasts between 4.47 and 5.67 seconds (personal communication with Tony Ashton), and therefore, the primary physical requirement is power. In recent international matches, the speed of many rucks has become much quicker, and this will likely continue. Because each match has over 100 rucks and mauls (International Rugby Board 2008), staying effective in the ruck for the full length of the match depends on both strength endurance and cardiorespiratory endurance.

Fitness Training Categories for Rugby

When planning your players' training and choosing from the games, drills, and activities in this book, keep in mind the time the ball is in play plus the length of phases and the periods between phases. Plan for the long term by using different work and rest lengths and work-to-rest ratios at different phases within the training year.

Lacking the fitness level needed for meeting the ever-changing demands of the game will lead to fatigue, which may lead to reduced skill accuracy and decision-making ability. Skill reduction has been shown in studies on soccer players (Stone et al. 2009), and the same is likely true with rugby players. Therefore, you must equip your players with the tools necessary for competing successfully on the field. Because rugby is such a multi-faceted game, your players will need field training that improves both their cardiorespiratory endurance and their agility. Collisions are tiring, and players need to have the strength to compete and dominate. The following sections address each fitness component.

Cardiorespiratory Fitness and Stamina

A typical rugby league player uses up to 6,800 kilojoules of energy per match, roughly 10 percent more than a soccer or rugby union player. According to Mike Gleeson of Loughborough University (2005), the most energetic players are halfbacks, centres, and fullbacks in rugby league and forwards in rugby union. Time and motion studies have measured the total distances covered by players in various positions as well as players' movements and the intensities of those movements.

Time and motion studies have revealed that a large percentage of match play is performed at lower intensities (Reilly and Gilbourne 2003). Consequently, the aerobic system makes the most significant contribution to energy delivery during team-sport play. Therefore, a rugby player needs a sufficiently developed aerobic system. Match analyses in soccer showed that increased aerobic fitness (Coutts and Abt 2005) did the following:

- Increased work intensity during the match
- Prevented a second-half reduction in work during the match
- Doubled the number of sprints completed in a match
- Allowed players to be involved in more decisive plays
- Allowed players to cover a greater distance during a match

Unlike running events, rugby involves a number of short-duration multi-directional runs. The amount of time and the distances rugby players run depend on their positions; this is particularly true of rugby union. Generally, outside backs cover the greatest distances during matches. When running at high speeds, players cover distances ranging from 3 to 34 metres. The average high-speed run for forwards and halfbacks spans about 8 metres; for outside backs, the average is 16 metres (Thomas 2003). The Cunniffe study (Cunniffe, Proctor, Baker, and Davies 2009) revealed that the forwards spent less of their time standing and walking than did the backs (66 vs. 78 percent) but had more slow-speed activities (315 vs. 229). Players covered an average distance of 19.7 metres in 87 moderate-intensity runs (>14 km/h). These data are similar to those of top-class soccer players, who perform 2 to 3 kilometres of high-intensity running (>15 km/h) (Iaua, Rampinini, and Bangsbo 2009). Average distances of 15.3 and 17.3 metres were recorded for backs and forwards, respectively, in sprint activities (>20 km/h; because the forwards were not split into further subgroups, this may not reflect true positional differences).

These studies show that the sprint distances covered in rugby union are very position specific, which has implications for training. The same is true for rugby league, but the differences are less marked. Rugby union test match data show that back three players (wings and fullback) perform over 40 high-speed runs (i.e., with speeds in excess of 5.5 metres per second) within the 40-minute ball-in-play time within a match. With 15 to 20 contact events per game also inducing fatigue, the importance of good speed endurance cannot be over-estimated for rugby players. The particular type of running fitness required for rugby must be trained for (i.e., training must improve acceleration, deceleration, and change of direction speed). Rugby league matches have a change in activity (e.g., tackle, sprint, change in direction) every four to six seconds. The intermittent stop-start nature of the running in team sports is far more physically demanding than running at a steady pace (Drust, Reilly, and Cable 2000).

Most aerobic training methods involve the whole body. They range from traditional running to more gym-based activities such as rowing, swimming, and cycling. Any activity that elevates the heart rate to approximately 60 to 80 percent of its maximum level for a sustained period (20 to 40 minutes) builds aerobic endurance. This type of steady-state training is useful for the general population and may be used during the teenage years as part of a programme to build the engine, but it is not at all specific to rugby. Interval training is much more relevant for rugby players because of the intermittent nature of the sport. (See the sidebar Interval Training for Rugby for more information.)

Related to cardiorespiratory fitness is stamina, or work capacity, which refers to players' ability to maintain their work rate throughout a match. This is not the same as the stamina that distance runners need. Rugby players need to be able to cover the required distances, play for 80 minutes, and also compete in the contact activities that are discussed later in the chapter.

Skill-based conditioning games simulate the movement patterns of team sports, while maintaining a competitive environment in which athletes must perform under pressure and when fatigued (Gabbett 2006). However, these games have to be well planned and organised to create the correct training effect.

Interval Training for Rugby

Interval training consists of a series of high-intensity activities (>80 percent HRmax) over a specified distance or time with a set recovery time between them. It produces aerobic as well as anaerobic benefits, leading to improvements in speed and efficiency under fatigue, as demonstrated in a recent study on soccer (Helgerud et al. 2001).

Rugby players must be able to cope with aerobic work interspersed with highly intense anaerobic work (e.g., chasing back after a line break and then defending in scrambling mode against the attacking team, repeatedly tackling and regaining one's feet, continuously mauling, and then running to the next breakdown and repeating). Once their aerobic fitness is at an acceptable level, players need to focus on improving their anaerobic threshold.

Anaerobic threshold can be improved through quite short, very intensive intervals and also longer, slightly less intensive intervals. Balsom and Soderlund (1999) recommended working at 90 percent HRmax for two to four minutes and resting for anywhere from 30 seconds to two minutes between work intervals. Longer intensive endurance methods can also be used once or twice a week, particularly earlier in the training phase. Longer endurance workouts take 8 to 15 minutes and include four or five blocks, or intervals. Here intensity is at 85 to 90 percent HRmax. Recovery time is about five minutes.

Numerous studies have examined the effects of high-intensity training on performance and adaptations in other sports. A review of high intensity training in soccer recommended running interval exercises at an intensity of 90 to 95 percent HRmax for three to eight minutes (Iaua, Rampinini, and Bangsbo 2009). A study in badminton showed the benefit of adding short, high intensity sport-related sprint activities (Walklate et al 2009).

The available evidence clearly shows that interval training is best for rugby players. Interval training bouts that are very short (less than 30 seconds) at a very high intensity with short rest periods primarily address the anaerobic system, although evidence suggests that intervals of this length also provide an appropriate aerobic stimulus (Bishop 2001). Longer bouts (two to ten minutes) stress both the anaerobic and aerobic pathways with greater emphasis on the latter.

As stated before, the work intensities, work intervals, and rest periods have to be carefully managed; but the bigger question is what to put in the work and rest periods. One of the key principles of training is specificity. For rugby players, this means running. However, running in a straight line for three minutes does not mimic the patterns of the game. Specificity can be increased with a rugby-specific drill or activity (e.g., passing drills, hitting tackle bags). Drills like these address the specific movement patterns and skills of the game; however, many do not involve decision making. Games are a more specific form of rugby training.

The University of Technology, Sydney recently conducted a study that compared the influence of adding extra high-intensity small-sided games or the equivalent amount of time doing interval training to the normal routine of female touch football players (Coutts and Sirotic 2004). In this study, both the interval training group and the small games group completed five to seven four-minute efforts at approximately 90 percent of maximum heart rate (HRmax) with three minutes of rest between efforts. After three weeks of training, aerobic fitness performance measured during match simulation (measured on a non-motorised treadmill) was improved by 10 percent in both the small games training group and the interval training group. As a general guide, completing between 15 and 30 minutes of high-intensity exercise (either interval training or small games training) and keeping athletes' heart rates above 90 percent HRmax should be sufficient for increasing fitness (Coutts and Abt 2005).

Strength and Power

Since the onset of full-time professionalism in both rugby union and rugby league, strength levels have increased; today's players are stronger than players of previous eras. In 1993, professional rugby league backs had 1RM bench scores of 113.1 kilograms, and forwards had scores of 119 (Meir 1993). In 1996, backs scored 106 kilograms, halfs scored 100.1, back row players scored 112.4, props scored 123.4, and hookers scored 99.7 (O'Connor 1996). An average of 134.8 was reported in 2001 (Baker 2001), and 142.7 was reported across all players in 2004 (Baker and Newton 2004).

Today's professional rugby players also exhibit higher power levels than earlier players did. National Rugby League (NRL) players were significantly more powerful in every variable measured than student rugby league players were, and the load at which their maximum power occurred was also significantly higher (Baker 2001). This has had a particular effect on the nature of rugby at the top level which is not necessarily reflected in the community, recreational level. This has particular relevance to the tackle area, in which the more experienced player is likely to be more powerful against an opponent than is the novice player. Also, 'results indicate that the difference in power output between teams of different playing levels may depend largely on differences in maximal strength' (Baker 2001).

As players become more experienced, their strength training focus changes. Initially, they increase power by increasing their absolute load while maintaining movement speed. However, once they have attained a base level of maximum strength and further large gains in strength are less likely to occur, increasing the load may not be the best strategy for increasing power. Rather, power is increased by increasing the speed at which each load is lifted (Baker 2001).

Players can use the major multi-joint lifts used in powerlifting and Olympic weightlifting, as well as other more rugby-specific rotational and strongman-type lifts, to improve strength in the gym. Partner body weight exercises around the tackle, ruck, maul, and play-the-ball, as well as supporting exercises derived from wrestling and grapple sports, were thought to contribute significantly to the increase in power of NRL players in a one-year period (Baker 2001). To be successful, players at every level of the sport need all of these forms of strength training. Some rugby and grapple exercises can be practised 'bone on bone,' whereas others will involve players with tackle suits. Exercises using tackle shields, tackle bags, and wrestling dummies can also be used. The set pieces of rugby union also require training time. Strength training is not the scope of this book, and apart from bag and shield activities, will not be discussed further.

Speed and Agility

Within phase play, speed is important to gain an advantage over the opponents (e.g., chasing kicks, supporting line breaks, and chasing down opponents). The particular aspect of speed that is most important is acceleration, because rugby players, for the most part, run short distances. This linked to the player's body mass, i.e., his momentum, is a key factor. (I think this point is important as a fast 140 pound player would not make it to the top level.

Speed is not the same for a rugby player as it is for a sprinter. Therefore, the training methods for the two sports differ. A good rugby sprinter 'has excellent acceleration, reaches top speed early, has outstanding balance and agility, avoids injury during impact, and is not affected unduly by carrying a ball' (Sayers 2000). A track sprinter, on the other hand, runs 100 metres in a straight line as quickly as possible. Rugby players rarely run in a straight line, and the ability to change direction rapidly (i.e., agility) is more important than top speed.

Rugby players also follow different cues than sprinters do, who respond only to the sound of the gun. Rugby players choose lines of running to outwit defenders, to support the running lines of their own players, to avoid defenders, and to collide with defenders as effectively as possible. Because they must change direction so often, rugby players typically have a running style that includes a forward leaning trunk, a lower centre of gravity, and a lower knee lift. Sprint coaches may criticise rugby players' style of running; however, the best rugby players have most likely achieved this status because of the way they run, rather than in spite of it.

Speed and agility are also needed for keeping the ball alive in contact. The ability to hit and spin and pass out of the tackle is associated with a high body mass and agility, as is the ability to beat a player: The ability to beat a player is significantly associated with high vertical jump height, fast agility, and 20- and 40-metre speeds. In addition, the ability to perform well in a 2v1 situation is significantly associated with fast agility (Gabbett, Kelly, and Pezet 2007).

Agility is defined as the ability to change direction with a minimum loss of pace (in rugby this means a minimum loss of forward velocity). However, this definition does not take into consideration any technical or tactical element. Sheppard and Young (2006) defined agility as 'a rapid, whole-body movement with a change of velocity in response to a stimulus' (Gabbett 2008).

Some players appear to possess exceptional agility, being able to 'beat a player on a sixpence,' or take the ball to the line and stand defenders up. What are the physical and mental characteristics that result in such agility? Does it depend on speed of foot, speed of thought, innate ability, or learnt responses? A recent literature review of agility articles revealed that agility performance does not appear to be strongly linked with straight speed components (Baker and Nance 1999; Buttifant, Graham, and Cross, 2002; Tsitskarsis, Theoharopoulus, and Garefis 2003; Young, Hawken, and McDonald 1996). Essentially, speed and agility are distinct physical qualities, and speed training does not appear to enhance change of direction speed (CODS), and CODS training does not appear to enhance speed (Young, McDowell, and Scarlett 2001). Therefore, training for change of direction speed and agility must involve highly specific training that recognises the specific demands of the sport.

Strength and power have always been thought to be major factors in determining agility, although this may not be as simple as once thought. It would appear that strength and power measures have an influence on change of direction speed (Negrete and Brophy 2000), but this relationship might only be observable over short distances. One might then infer that in sports such as badminton and field sport positions that involve changes of direction over short distances (e.g., soccer goalkeeping), strength and power measures have a stronger relationship with change of direction speed than they would in sport positions that require directional changes with higher speeds over longer distances (e.g., soccer forwards). However, this is not entirely clear.

Strength training alone, however, will not improve sport-specific agility. Based on the results of Djevalikian (1993), Webb and Lander (1983), and Young and colleagues (1996, 2002), concentric strength and power measures appear to be poor predictors of change of direction speed, which indicates the need to work specifically on the other components that determine agility. Many rugby players tend to be deficient in controlled eccentric strength. From this we should conclude that strength and power are important but not exclusive factors in directional changes within rugby because most directional changes take place after travelling relatively short distances. Given the importance of strength and power in improving acceleration and in dominating the collision, the role of strength training cannot be overstated.

A lack of general fitness is often reflected in poor body composition scores. Test batteries have revealed that athletes in sports such as rugby and soccer who perform well on CODS tests tend to have lower body fat levels (Gabbett et al 2007; Meir et al. 2001; Reilly et al. 2000; Rigg and Reilly 1987). This is of particular relevance when working with recreational players. The best way to initially improve agility in recreational players may be to increase endurance, thereby improving body composition.

Activities to improve agility can be either planned or random. Planned, or programmed, agility activities can involve having players run pre-determined patterns through equipment such as cones and ladders, or run specific lines. However, more common in team sports are reactive agility situations that cannot be pre-planned.

Studies show that simple planned agility activities improve coordination and efficiency of movement. However, the value of having the whole team practise planned agility movements is questionable. You need to achieve a balance between planned agility to improve basic biomechanics and reactive agility to increase players' abilities to react to gamelike situations.

The use of cones in agility training is questionable because players can pre-plan their movements around them. This does not reflect the reality of match situations, which require players to react to a changing environment. The transfer of skill from a cone agility drill to a match would therefore be minimal.

Recently, there has been an influx of products that purport to develop agility by requiring players to respond quickly. We have yet to see flashing lights or directional arrows on the playing field, and hence this form of training is not transferable. A more valuable method of developing reactive agility is small-sided or conditioned games. Such games allow players to experience all the change of direction situations and perceptual information sources that occur in the real game (Bruce, Farrow, and Young 2004).

Rugby union and league are both highly skilled multi-faceted sports requiring many technical and physical skills. Improving general strength is important for athletic development and injury prevention and should be started at an early age. High maximum strength and power levels are important to control the collisions. Specific types of power and static strength are required to dominate in the set pieces of rugby union. More rugby-specific strength training such as strongman and grappling should also be included.

A moderately high level of aerobic endurance plus a high level of anaerobic endurance are required to sustain the demands of repeated high-intensity efforts such as sprinting, tackling, rucking, and mauling. Rugby is multi-directional and requires acceleration and deceleration in a multitude of directions from various starting positions. Added to this is the need to read the game by anticipating and responding accurately to changing cues. You can improve your players' endurance and agility by offering them rugby-specific movement patterns in the forms of drills and pre-planned activities that enhance the energy systems required to play the game. However, to complete their armoury, you will need to include games designed to improve both physical fitness and game sense.

CHAPTER 10

Planning for the Season

The old cliché 'Failure to plan is planning to fail' contains a large degree of truth. Like your players, you need to plan for improvement. Before you plan, however, you should assess your players' current performance and the strengths and weaknesses of your team and individual players.

Your assessment should include rugby-specific technical and tactical areas as well as physical components such as speed, agility, strength, power, and endurance. This assessment will enable you to plan for the season ahead, agree on goals with your team and individual players, and design programmes to improve the physical and technical aspects of individual players which will benefit the team as a whole. Be sure to do this in cooperation with other members of your staff, keeping in mind that it will require more sophistication at higher levels of performance.

Season Planning

Season planning can be done by breaking down the time available into workable phases, depending on the time of year. These are typically known as the off-season, pre-season, and in-season. Within a yearly cycle are distinct phases, which are often referred to as the general preparation phase (off-season); the specific preparation phase (pre-season); the pre-competition phase (i.e., pre-season games); the competition phase (in-season); and finally, the transition phase (many consider this part of their off-season). You will have specific targets and aims depending on the phase of the training year and the requirements of your team.

The first thing you should do for each phase of the rugby season is determine the following:

- Aims and goals
- Start and end points
- Progression
- Adjustments for players' needs
- Methods of measuring the efficacy of the programme

Aims and Goals

Depending on the level of competition and your players' abilities, typically, the aims and goals cover technical and tactical skills and fitness components such as speed, strength, and endurance as well as additional factors such as psychology and nutrition. You will want to take into account the goals for each of these areas when planning individual practice sessions within the context of the phase of the season you are in (we'll talk more about planning practices in the next section, "Practice Planning," beginning on page 172).

Conditioners at any level, and coaches working alone at recreational levels, should focus on technical skills, tactics, and the elements of rugby fitness. Consider the sample yearly training plan in figure 10.1. Your team's training objectives of each particular phase can be planned here, and the general aims will be filled in. You will want to adapt your objectives to the situation at hand as your team progresses through its pre-season and playing programme.

FIGURE 10.1 Yearly Training Plan*

Month	Technical skills	Tactical skills	Fitness	Ancillary (psychological, nutrition, etc.)
1	*Off-season (weeks 1-4):* Handling contact and kicking skills	*Off-season (weeks 1-4):* General principles of offence and defence	*Off-season (weeks 1-4):* General aerobic improvement through games and intervals; general strength training and hypertrophy	*Off-season (weeks 1-4):* Weighing and general dietary advice
2	*Off-season (weeks 1-2):* Handling contact and kicking skills	*Off-season (weeks 1-2):* General principles of offence and defence	*Off-season (weeks 1-2):* General aerobic improvement through games and intervals; general strength training, hypertrophy, and individual injury prevention programs	*Off-season (weeks 1-2):* Weighing and general dietary advice
	Pre-season (weeks 3-4): Group and position-specific skills	*Pre-season (weeks 3-4):* Team tactics and building principles into scenarios	*Pre-season (weeks 3-4):* Rugby-specific aerobic and anaerobic training through games and intervals. More rugby-specific strength training involving maximum strength and power development	*Pre-season (weeks 3-4):* Individual and team goal setting
3	*Pre-season (weeks 1-2):* Group and position-specific skills	*Pre-season (weeks 1-2):* Team tactics and building principles into scenarios	*Pre-season (weeks 1-2):* Rugby-specific aerobic and anaerobic training through games and intervals. More rugby-specific strength training involving maximum strength and power development	*Pre-season (weeks 1-2):* Individual and team goal setting
	Pre-competition (weeks 3-4): Games	*Pre-competition (weeks 3-4):* Games	*Pre-competition (weeks 3-4):* Games	*Pre-competition (weeks 3-4):* Games
4-12	*In-season:* Maintenance and team technical skills. Remedial work on individual skills. Progressive programme to develop core skills each week	*In-season:* Progressive programme to develop tactical skills each week. Also, remedial work on previous week	*In-season:* Maintenance of strength with two gym sessions per week. Maintenance of aerobic and anaerobic fitness with two sessions of 15-30 minutes per week as part of rugby session. Strength and fitness to be planned throughout the year in waves with high- and low-load weeks. Some maximal speed to be done for backs each week. Agility for all players as part of rugby sessions	*In-season:* Regular reviews of individual and team goals. Regular advice on hydration, diet, and body composition

*For a full-time professional player, strength training will take place at the club. For a part-time professional player or student, some of the strength sessions may take place at the club and some away from the club in the player's own time. For a recreational player, strength training will be done away from the club in the player's own time. Note also that speed and agility have not been included, as for a recreational team this will form part of the main rugby session.

Start and End Points

In conjunction with your players and the staff, you will determine the start and end points from season to season by assessing where the team is both technically and physically. This will help you, your staff, and the players set goals to achieve during the next season. Physical components such as speed, endurance, and strength can be measured using simple field and gym tests. Because technical and tactical qualities are more difficult to measure objectively, determine what key elements you want to address.

After the season ends, the players typically have one or two weeks of complete rest followed by an additional one or two weeks of non-specific cross-training for maintaining general fitness. Your players' age, experience level, injury status, and life circumstances will determine the length and nature of this period (also known as the transition phase).

After this transition phase, the players begin the general preparation phase, or off-season, during which they may work away from the club. An example might be three strength sessions at a gym and three cardiorespiratory sessions at a gym or on grass per week. An alternative for recreational players may be to play sports such as basketball or racket sports.

Players normally report back to club training in the second half of the general preparation phase, at which point they undergo basic field-based fitness tests. These give you the opportunity to judge the general fitness of the team and also to highlight individual player deficiencies and offer advice. In the general preparation phase, you will want to improve general aerobic condition via games and intervals, and then test this fitness component at the end of the phase. You may also be trying to improve players' core skills and may analyse their improvement using video analysis. You may aim to improve more rugby-specific anaerobic endurance during the pre-season and may test for this at the start and end of the specific preparation phase.

Progression

When planning a programme of work over a short block of time, you must ensure that the sessions are progressive and linked. When planning individual sessions, make sure the activities progress to improve players' technical skills and fitness, and that each session builds on the previous sessions. An understanding of the principles of training will help you build progressive overload into your sessions—in terms of volume or intensity depending on the phase of the year. This overload applies to technical and tactical skill as well as to aspects of fitness.

Improving a particular skill or physical component requires a week-to-week increase in volume, intensity, or complexity. Volume refers to the time spent practising the particular skill or the length of time spent on particular fitness activities. The intensity at which players practise skills can be governed by the nature of the opposition within the activity, or the amount of decision making involved. In pure fitness drills, intensity refers to the speed of work, the recovery time, or the time spent in particular heart rate zones (this can also be used to measure volume).

You can also progress the complexity of the technical skill or the tactical awareness involved. To progress the mental component, add more intense competition, reduce the decision-making time within games, or make the games more complex and chaotic (i.e., more matchlike). Resist the temptation to increase all of these in a short period of time. Good coaches understand that they cannot overload all aspects at once; rather, they prioritise one or two areas in which they want their players to improve. For example, at the recreational level, practice sessions during the off-season emphasise improvements in technical skill and aerobic endurance, whereas the practice sessions during the pre-season usually focus on anaerobic endurance and tactical skill. If you are a recreational coach, your progressive practices during the off-season may look like those in figure 10.2.

Adjustments for Players' Needs

When planning for the phases of the season, you must know your players, including their age, their physical and mental maturity levels, their experience (training age), the diversity of the group, and how they been coached in the past, if at all. To plan each session well, you must consider your own characteristics, your players, and the content. Your own characteristics consist of your knowledge, strengths, weaknesses, and delivery style. Next, consider the age, experience, and maturity level of your players. What coaching delivery style

FIGURE 10.2 Practice Progression During the Off-Season

	Session 1	Session 2	Session 3	Session 4
Goal	Introduction to the training block, practising fast hands and support	Practising support and performing fitness drills	Building volume and increasing rugby-specific fitness games	Increasing intensity by adding two-touch support rule
Main content	• Warm-up using ball skills games and general mobility (15 min.) • Rugby strength and agility drills (15 min.) • 6v3+3 (3 min.) • 2v1 closed skill activity (3 min.) • Fitness building made up of 2 × 8 min. of 8v8 Offside Touch with 4 min. recovery between games • Cool-down (5 min.) followed by mobility exercises (two sets at 2 min. each)	• Warm-up using ball skills games and general mobility (15 min.) • Rugby strength and agility drills (15 min.) • 6v4 Rotation (3 min.) • 2v1+1 (3 min.) • Fitness building made up of 2 × 8 min. of 8v8 Offside Touch with 4 min. recovery, plus 10 × 40 m sprints on a 30 s turnaround • Cool-down (5 min.) followed by mobility exercises (three sets at 2 min. each)	• Warm-up using ball skills games and general mobility (15 min.) • Rugby strength and agility drills (15 min.) • 6v4 Rotation (3 min.) • 3v2+2 (3 min.) • Fitness building made up of 5 × 4 min. of Playmaker Attack with 2 min. recovery, plus 20 × 40 m sprints on a 30 s turnaround • Cool-down (5 min.) followed by mobility exercises (three sets at 3 min. each)	• Warm-up using ball skills games and general mobility (15 min.) • Rugby strength and agility drills (15 min.) • Overload Touch (3 min.) • 3v2+2 (3 min.) • Fitness building made up of 6 × 3 min. of 10v8 Two-Tackle Offside Touch or Offload Touch with 1 min. recovery, plus 20 × 40 m sprints on a 30 s turnaround • Cool-down (5 min.) followed by mobility exercises (three sets at 4 min. each)

would best meet the needs of your players? With this information in mind, plan the content of your sessions to match the needs of your players, your own strengths, and the environment in which you will be coaching (i.e., indoors, outdoors on grass, outdoors on artificial surfaces, or a mixture). Meticulous season planning is one of the key components of success.

Watch your players perform before you start planning the programme, and ask the players for their views. At this point you can determine your priorities: the key skills and fitness components to develop and the coaching method that would be appropriate for this particular group of players.

Measuring the Efficacy of the Programme

Once you have a plan in place, you must determine whether it is organised, accurate, and deliverable. Are the sessions pitched at the appropriate level? Do the sessions progress? Does your programme address various needs? Will the programme maintain players' interest? Although this last question is particularly important at the recreational and school levels, where players attend voluntarily, it also applies to elite levels, where players still benefit from enjoyable and relevant sessions. Your methods of measuring your programme will depend on your players' age, their commitment level, and their skill levels and fitness standards. Here are a few examples:

- For very young children, you might use a simple traffic light system at the end of each session to find out whether they enjoyed the session. The children place round pieces of cardboard that show a smiley green face, a neutral amber face, or a stern red face into a box to communicate how they felt about the session. Use this system in conjunction with a log in which you check off either *achieved* or *has not achieved* for each child in each session.
- At the recreational club level, you can use simple field tests to measure improvements in fitness, and closed skill tests or of film footage of training to measure improvements in technical skills.
- At the professional level, you will use a wide battery of field- and lab-based tests to measure improvements in physical components. Improvements in technical and tactical skills are evaluated using training film footage, observations of practice games, and various statistical software packages that measure the involvement of the player in terms of number of tackles, ball carries, etc.

Practice Planning

A traditional training session typically includes a warm-up, skills practice using drills, and a cool-down. This method can be very well organised and enjoyable, but all too often, the warm-up is not specific to rugby and involves players lapping the pitch and then doing static stretches. The skills drills are then often very static with very little transfer to the game, and players often spend a lot of time standing around waiting their turn. The problem with this approach is that players want to play, not to drill. This traditional approach is not very enjoyable for players, has a low level of player involvement, and does not transfer well to the real game.

An alternative model using the games approach structures a practice session with a warm-up that includes a game, followed by a game to develop technical and tactical understanding and a discussion of how players could have been better tactically, perceptually, and in their decision making. At this point, players go back to the game (or a more advanced progression of the game if they are competent), and repeat the game sense cycle. The session ends with a cool-down. Of course, if necessary, a games approach practice session can include closed skill drills if further refining of a technical skill or aspect of play is needed. This adheres to the whole-part-whole concept.

An important aspect of the games approach is the role you take in relation to your players. Traditionally, training sessions have been coach dominated, with players being told where to stand, how to defend a situation, and so on. The emphasis of the games approach is on the players making decisions rather than the coach. Your role is that of a facilitator who creates situations in which players have to come up with solutions for themselves (i.e., problem solving). (For a more detailed account of the process of empowerment see pages 16 and 17 of Kidman's *Developing Decision Makers: An Empowerment Approach to Coaching* or Ray Maclean's *Any Given Team*).

Components of a Games Approach Practice Session

The games approach practice is, as the title implies, largely delivered through the medium of games. The practice has a theme, and the games within the session should be designed to address that theme. In the first part of the practice, the whole team is split into small groups that play small-sided games. Because these games are familiar to the players, they require minimal instruction. The small number of players on each team maximises player involvement and also leads to good communication among players. Later in the session, games that are less familiar to the players can be used to challenge technical and tactical awareness. Decide whether any of these games are purely for conditioning, as well as the work-to-rest ratios and intensities. You can use specific breakout drills to have players practise specific skills in a more isolated way if required. Create a practice plan using a template such as the one shown in figure 10.3 so that you have a general overview of the session before it begins.

Warm-Up

The first part of the practice session is used to warm the players up both physically and mentally. The physical warm-up is primarily used as injury prevention. The first activities might be quite low key and progressively increase players' heart rates to cause more blood to flow, thus warming up the muscles and joints. When this has happened, the joints can be safely moved through a greater range of motion using the movement patterns that are used in the game. Depending on the activities to follow, warm-ups last from 10 to 30 minutes, with most being around 20 minutes.

Games or drills that involve maximum speed require the longest warm-up. Sessions that will involve tackling and other forms of contact require the upper body as well as the lower body to be warmed up. In the games approach, small-sided non-specific games can be used in the first part of the warm-up to raise players' heart rates; they are also used to add a component of fun, aid communication, and introduce a competitive element.

FIGURE 10.3 Sample Practice Plan Template		
	Activity	**Coaching points**
Warm-up		
Main session		
Cool-down		

From Rugby Football Union, 2012, *Rugby games & drills* (Champaign, IL: Human Kinetics).

Some drills can be used following a general and dynamic warm-up to develop speed and agility in a game-related context, provided adequate rest intervals are taken.

After the small-sided games, the next part of the warm-up should include dynamic flexibility exercises (e.g., running and skipping drills), followed by games in a larger area to allow players to stride out more and increase their running speed. After this, players can perform another set of dynamic flexibility exercises, possibly in a stationary position so you can talk to the team.

Main Session

The players should now be ready to participate in the main part of the session, which contains the main activities designed for achieving the goals identified for that part of the training programme. These goals are technical, tactical, and physical. If the session includes a section on speed and agility, have players do this first. Bag drills with a work period of less than one minute may be included here (e.g., Y Drill on page 72, Zigzag Runs on page 69, and Cover and Chase on page 63), as long as you observe the correct work-to-rest ratios. If the players are going to do any continuous work for longer than a minute using bag drills or shuttle runs, have them do these at the end of the session for 10 to 15 minutes. This part of the main session typically lasts for 10 to 20 minutes.

At the recreational level, you do not have the luxury of seeing your players more than two or three times a week. Therefore, they will need to do some rugby-specific strength training at the start of the main session as well. Although you may not include this every session, when you do, have players do it when they are quite fresh. This type of work includes player-on-player tackling and wrestling drills plus activities such as tyre flipping. This part of the main session typically lasts for 10 to 15 minutes.

Once your players have completed any speed, agility, and rugby-specific strength work, commence the main part of the session. The session can include two to four games based on a particular theme. For example, if a session is primarily aimed at improving fitness, use activities that the players are familiar with so there is less input required from you and more continuous work on the part of the players. If the session is primarily to develop the technical and tactical aspects of rugby, the players should be presented with more difficult rugby situations within the games. You may also use some smaller static and enclosed drills to reiterate certain coaching points using the whole-part-whole approach.

This part of the main session typically lasts anywhere from 30 to 60 minutes. Of course, proficient teams intersperse highly technical and tactical games with very demanding running or rugby strength exercises to fatigue the players and further test their rugby skills under pressure. This approach should not be used with players whose fitness or skill levels (or both) are substandard because the quality of the sessions will almost certainly suffer and players' skills will not improve. Remember, do not increase the physical and the technical intensity at the same time when planning sessions.

When organising a practice's main session using a games approach, you must take a number of principles into account. The specificity of the games is very important; as explained earlier, there is a continuum from totally non-specific activities to a game under full rugby rules. Before introducing games to a session, look at the aims of the session (e.g., are the games being used as part of a technical session, to practise a skill in a matchlike situation, or as a conditioning tool?). If the session is purely a coaching session, (i.e. an educational session to develop technical and tactical skills), the rest periods may be long to allow you and your players to interact, and the activities themselves may not be that intense. To use games as conditioning tools, you need to consider where you are in the training year, the energy systems that the games address primarily, and how you will manipulate the work-to-rest ratios and the intensity to achieve your desired results. With these things in mind, consider the following principles:

- Smaller numbers of players in the same game will increase the intensity (generally, the highest-intensity games are played with six or fewer players per team).
- Smaller grids normally demand a greater number of changes in direction, and games with a large number of changes of direction are more demanding than games with fewer.
- Larger grids are required for players to achieve the maximum speeds attained in a match.
- Games of a very high intensity cannot be carried out for long periods of time, and the greater the intensity of the game, the longer the required rest period if the activity is to be repeated.

- Grids and groups must be well organised in advance, and fluid breaks should be controlled to maintain the correct work-to-rest ratios.
- The players should be relatively familiar with the game to keep explanation to a minimum.
- Games can be followed by light skills activities as a form of active recovery, or they can be followed by demanding fitness activities to heavily tax the anaerobic system. Games also can be preceded by these activities to pre-exhaust players to test their skills when fatigued.
- The skill levels and ages of your players must be taken into consideration. If the game is technically too demanding, the conditioning effect will be reduced because the game will break down.

An understanding of these principles and how they relate to the training phase your players are in and their age and ability levels will help you improve both their game understanding and their endurance. The games can be quite simple or more complicated to develop technical aspects of play. This is where the coach and conditioner must work together. To use games and game-related drills as the majority of your on-field conditioning and to make the best use of the time available, you must have an idea of where to put these in your training plan. You need to know how to manipulate the intensity of the various games to gain the required training effect. To do this, you must understand the predominant energy system that is stressed during the game or drill and its technical and tactical complexity. This will largely be determined by the length of time of the activity and the rest periods. Remember, as described in the fitness section, games lasting over four minutes are primarily for aerobic development, those lasting between two and four minutes are most appropriate for taxing players' aerobic systems and improving their anaerobic thresholds, and more demanding activities of a shorter duration overload the anaerobic system.

The classic periodisation model for developing cardiorespiratory fitness involves first improving aerobic endurance and then anaerobic endurance. The length of the games decrease though the pre-season from, say, three 8-minute games with 2 minutes of recovery to six 3-minute games with 1 minute of recovery plus six 1-minute games with 2 minutes of recovery. In the general preparation phase, two to three sessions of 45 to 60 minutes could be used. In the specific preparation phase, one session of 45 minutes could be used, and within the competition phase, one 15- to 30-minute session should suffice, depending on the fixture list and the make-up of the rest of the training week. This will depend upon the intensity of the previous game, the perceived intensity of the up and coming game and the physical demands of the activities planned in that particular training week. The games and activities also progress from less specific to more specific. During the competition phase, one intense session of between 15 and 30 minutes would suffice depending on the previous and forthcoming fixtures and the content of the training week.

Games can be made more physically demanding in a number of ways. You can require that your players get up and down from the floor, or run to specific points before being onside and back in the game. You can introduce various levels of contact to stop the ball carrier with a continuum from touching the player, to gripping, to gripping and holding, and gripping, holding and putting to ground to full contact. Depending on the nature of the game, the number of players or the size of the playing area can be altered. You can also increase physical pressure by having players defend for long periods of time, or defend their goal line, particularly with reduced numbers. Individual games can be altered slightly to adjust the technical pressure. Consider altering small-sided and large-sided games in terms of rules, player numbers, and pitch dimensions to change the technical focus.

Conditioning games can be an integral part of your yearly programme, improving the skill and performance of individual players, the team, or both. They can emphasise coordination and communication in defence, quality second-phase play, field positioning skills, and ball control (to name a few). The development of these games is limited only by your imagination. They can be designed to suit your workspace, with rules and field sizes modified to meet the physical demands and challenges placed on players in various positions. Ultimately, the goal of conditioning games is to develop tactically smarter players (Gabbett 2001). Because conditioning games empower players, they develop good decision makers and leaders and thus are part of a player-centred coaching approach.

When developing conditioning games, ask yourself the following questions:

- What aspect, tactic, or skill am I trying to develop with this game?
- What modifications or exaggerations can I make to best set up this situation?
- Can I borrow aspects of another sport to enhance this game?
- What are the key questions I need to ask the players?
- Am I catering for all players? Do I need to give some choices in equipment and skill execution?
- How will I place the game within the training session?
- What progressions can I make to increase the complexity?
- Can I give the players some choices in these progressions?

Cool-Down

Players must cool down properly after the main rugby session. This should involve a return to activities of a lower intensity, such as non-competitive passing. Some low-intensity dynamic movements such as leg swings and hip rotations can follow this. Finally, players can do some simple static stretches, particularly for the legs. If possible, cool-down activities and stretches can be carried out in a swimming pool.

Sample Practice Plans

Let's take a look at a few examples of practice plans that focus on different phases and areas of play. The first four plans are for certain phases of the recreational training year: general preparation (off-season; see figure 10.4), specific preparation (pre-season; see figure 10.5), pre-competition (see figure 10.6), and competition (in-season; see figure 10.7).

FIGURE 10.4 Sample General Preparation (Off-Season) Practice Plan

	Activity	Coaching points
Warm-up	• Fifth Columnist (p. 28), 4 min. • Mobility exercises (e.g., high knees and heel kicks), 2 min. • End Corner Ball (p. 30), 4 min. on/1 min. off • Mobility exercises (e.g., lateral shuffles and cariocas) and upper-body exercises, 2 min.	• Encourage communication among team-mates. • Use these games to develop accurate passing. • Ensure that players hold and catch the ball correctly. • Ensure that players mobilise the key joints through an increased range of movement.
Main session	**Speed and Agility** • Y Drill (p. 72), 5 min. • Zigzag Runs (bag drill) (p. 69), 5 min. **Rugby-Specific Strength** • One-on-one tackle technique, 10 min. **High-Intensity Energy System Development** • Offside Touch (p. 93), 12 min. • Base Cone Touch (p. 139), 12 min. • Individual passing technique for accuracy, 10-15 min.	• Encourage players to chop their stride before contact and accelerate and decelerate around the bags. • Ensure that players maintain an athletic low body position with chest over knees over toes. • For Offside Touch, ensure that players work off the ball to get into a good space to receive a pass. • For Base Cone Touch, ensure that the attacking team attacks spaces left by the defenders and exploits the 2v1 situations created. • For Base Cone Touch, ensure that defenders work hard to get back into the defensive line.
Cool-down	• Line passing in groups of four in which players line up 5 m apart across a 15-m grid, 4 min. • Seated static stretches for hamstrings, quadriceps, hip flexors, and calves, 5 min.	• Ensure that players maintain passing accuracy in the cool-down period. • Have players hold each stretch for a minimum of 15 s.

FIGURE 10.5 Sample Specific Preparation (Pre-Season) Practice Plan

	Activity	Coaching points
Warm-up	• 4v4 One-Tackle Touch (p. 112), 4 min. on/1 min. off • Mobility exercises (e.g., high knees and heel kicks, skipping) 2-5 min. • Grid 4v3 (p. 114), 4 × 2 min. • Mobility exercises (e.g., lateral shuffles and cariocas; skipping with internal/external rotation) and upper-body exercises, 2-5 min.	• Ensure that players make accurate passes. • Ensure that players exploit the 2v1 situations that are created. • For Grid 4v3, ensure that the defence works hard, communicates, and maintains defensive unity and alignment.
Main session	**Speed and Agility** • Y Drill in pairs (p. 72), 5 min. • Slide and Realign (p. 76), 5 min. **Rugby-Specific Strength** • 2v1 tackle technique, 10 min. **Speed Endurance** • Readjustment to defend tight spots, 10 min. **High-Intensity Energy System Development** • Triple Overload Touch (p. 138), 10 min. • Base Cone Touch (p. 139), 10 min. • Technical and tactical breakout work for team offence, 10-15 min.	• Ensure that the defenders maintain defensive shape and work hard as a unit. • Ensure that all players communicate with each other. • Players must maintain good shoulder contact and foot placement prior to contact. • Encourage accurate passing and patience for the attacking team. • Encourage the defence to work hard to readjust and slide or drift when short of numbers.
Cool-down	• Line passing in groups of four, in which players line up 5 m apart across a 15-m grid, 4 min. • Seated static stretches for hamstrings, quadriceps, hip flexors, and calves, 5 min.	• Ensure that players maintain passing accuracy in the cool-down period. • Have players hold each stretch for a minimum of 15 s.

FIGURE 10.6 Sample Pre-Competition Phase Practice Plan

	Activity	Coaching points
Warm-up	• Keep Ball (p. 24), 4 × 1 min. on/1 min. off • Mobility exercises (e.g., front-to-back and side-to-side leg swings; alternating leg lunges), 2-5 min. • 6v4 Rotation (p. 118), 5 min. • Mobility exercises (e.g., squats, wood chops, forward and backward arm circles), 2-5 min.	• Encourage accurate passing. • Ensure that players work off the ball to get into space. • Ensure that all players communicate with each other. • Attackers must be patient and exploit 2v1 situations effectively when they occur. • Defenders must drift or slide as a unit.
Main session	**Speed and Agility** • Back and Maintain Shape (p. 75), 5 min. **Rugby-Specific Strength** • Ruck grapple technique, 10 min. **Speed Endurance** • Live Break Drill (p. 89), 10 min. **High-Intensity Energy System Development** • Out to In, In to Out (p. 150), 10 min. • Technical and tactical situational defence, 10-15 min.	• Insist on defensive unity and good speed of the defensive line. • Teach correct points about using levers in the grapple. • Ensure that defenders work hard to get back in defence and then work forward as a unit. • Encourage defenders to adopt the defensive pattern that suits the situation depending on their numbers in position on the pitch. • Ensure that defenders maintain a defensive shape and structure against various attacking situations.
Cool-down	• Mobility exercises (skipping, heel flicks) in groups of four, 4 min. • Seated static stretches for hamstrings, quadriceps, hip flexors, and calves, 5 min.	• Ensure that players maintain good form in the mobility exercises. • Have players hold each stretch for a minimum of 15 s.

FIGURE 10.7 Sample Competition Phase Practice Plan

	Activity	Coaching points
Warm-up	• One-Tackle Touch (p. 112), 4 × 1 min. on/1 min. off • Mobility exercises (e.g., front-to-back and side-to-side leg swings, alternating leg lunges), 2-5 min. • 6v6 Touch Overload (p. 121), 5 min. • Mobility exercises (e.g., squats, wood chops, forward and backward arm circles), 2-5 min.	• Encourage accurate passing. • Attackers must be patient and exploit 2v1 situations effectively when they occur. Defenders need to communicate and drift or slide as a unit.
Main session	**Speed and Agility** • Back and Maintain Shape (p. 75), 5 min. **Rugby-Specific Strength** • Ruck grapple technique, 10 min. • Technical and tactical practice (mix of games to highlight specific aspects that will be encountered in upcoming match), 40 min. **High-Intensity Energy System Development** • 6v3+3, 4 × 4 min., 1 min. recovery	• Encourage defensive unity and good speed of the defensive line. • Teach correct points about using levers in the grapple.
Cool-down	• Mobility exercises (skipping, heel flicks) in groups of four, 4 min. • Seated static stretches for hamstrings, quadriceps, hip flexors, and calves, 5 min.	• Ensure that players maintain good form in the mobility exercises. • Have players hold each stretch for a minimum of 15 s.

Most rugby sessions have a technical/tactical or team organisation component as well as a physical one; thus, in the previous examples, each session had a specific technical/tactical development part. This part of the session will probably not have a large fitness effect because of the time needed for you and your players to confer about the requirements involved. However, you can construct a session that primarily develops fitness in the context of a particular rugby theme. Three examples are provided: the first develops fitness using a defensive theme, the second has a handling and decision-making theme, and the third uses an offloading-in-contact theme.

In figure 10.7, groups of six players can be nominated and asked to put on bibs at the beginning of the session. In the first activity, they play against members of their own groups, or half of them play against half of the members of another group (i.e., 3v3 one tackle touch). In the second warm-up game, 6v6 touch overload is used. In the metabolic development games at the end, variations of 6v6 are used, or two groups join forces to form groups of 12 (6v3 + 3). If you are working with a team or squad for a season or tour, it may be worth your while to break the squad into smaller teams at

FIGURE 10.8 Sample Defensive Rugby-Specific Fitness-Based Practice Plan

	Activity	Coaching points
Warm-up	• One-Tackle Touch (p. 112), two groups at 3 × 1 min. for a total of 6 min. • Mobility exercises (e.g., heel flicks, backward running, lateral shuffles), 2 min. • Defensive Drift (p. 126), 6 min. • Mobility exercises (e.g., walking squats, alternating lunges, prone knee raises), 4 min.	• Encourage accurate passing and communication in attack. • Encourage the defence to work hard as a unit and communicate.
Main session	**Speed and Agility** • Slide and Realign (p. 76), 5 min. • Individual sprints and cuts with ball over position-specific distances, 5 min. **Speed Endurance** • Shuttles over various distances, 5 min. • Defensive line bag work, 5 min. **Rugby-Specific Strength** • 1v1 and 2v2 tackle technique, lifting and grappling, 10 min. **High-Intensity Energy System Development** • 6v4 Rotation (p. 118), 6 min. • Three-Colour Team Touch (p. 129), 8 min. • Three-Team Rotational Touch variation with tacklers on ground (p. 124), 6 min.	• Encourage the defence to work together as a unit. • Players must transfer the ball from two-hand to one-hand carries where required. • Encourage good foot placement, head position, and shoulder contact; players should finish with the arms and good leg drive. • Encourage good communication. • Defence must slide or drift when required.
Cool-down	• Passing in groups of four, 5 min. • Seated static stretches for hamstrings, quadriceps, hip flexors, and calves, 5 min.	• Ensure that players maintain accuracy of passes. • Have players hold each stretch for a minimum of 15 s.

the beginning of the season to encourage a competitive ethic and also ease session organisation.

A rugby conditioning session with a defensive focus may look like the one outlined in figure 10.8. This session is 68 minutes long plus turnover time, which is very tough. Normally, a session would not consist of so many components. The purpose of this figure is to illustrate the point that tough sessions must be organised in advance and run like clockwork so they flow. Also, organisation is much easier when you progress the games simply in your session.

A simple session using the same basic template with a theme to develop handling skills and decision making with an attacking overload may look like that in figure 10.9. This gives a total time of 52 minutes plus time between activities. If this session is primarily for developing fitness, the players must be competent and familiar with all of the activities so that a breakdown in skill does not affect intensity. Because of the length of time spent on fitness, these sessions (i.e., the defensive conditioning session and the handling decision-making session) would most appropriate for the specific pre-season preparation phase.

FIGURE 10.9   **Sample Handling and Decision-Making Rugby-Specific Fitness-Based Practice Plan**

	Activity	Coaching points
Warm-up	• Keep Ball (p. 24), three groups of 4v4 at 3 × 1 min. on/20 s off for total of 4 min. • Mobility exercises (e.g., alternating leg and arm raises from an all-fours position, supine leg raises, internal hip rotations), 2 min • Ball Tag (p. 27), three groups of 3v5 at 3 × 1 min. on/20 s off for total of 4 min. • Mobility exercises (e.g., wood chops, standing external hip rotations), 2 min.	• Encourage accuracy of passing and communication among attackers. • Encourage players to move off the ball and get into space.
Main session	**Speed and Agility** • 2v1+1 Drill (p. 52) with reload down one channel for a 1:6 work-to-rest, 5 min. **Speed Endurance** • 4v2+2 Drill (p. 57), three groups attack for 30 s with a 10 s turnaround for a total of 5 min. **Rugby-Specific Strength** • Ground work (player-on-player technique to control opponents on the ground at the breakdown), 10 min. **High-Intensity Energy System Development** • Touch Overload (p. 121), 10 min. • Base Cone Touch (p. 139), 10 min.	• Encourage accuracy of passing and communication among attackers. • Encourage ball carriers to fix or drag defenders. • Encourage players to maintain accuracy and decision making when fatigued. • Players must make use of levers and body position in lifts.
Cool-down	• Players line up in two lines for kicking and catching, 5 min. • Seated static stretches for hamstrings, quadriceps, hip flexors, and calves, 5 min.	• Players must keep moving and maintain accuracy of kicks and catches. • Have players hold each stretch for a minimum of 15 s.

You could use games in a session to work on a particular group of skills such as the hit and spin, the bump off, busting through, and running relevant running lines (i.e., attacking and offloading in the contact zone), as shown in figure 10.10. Before using these skills in games intended to develop fitness, make sure your players are proficient with them. The hit and spin is primarily used to obtain second phase by moving the ball quickly out of the contact situation and thereby keeping the attack alive. Therefore, the small-sided activities such as the Keep Ball Contact Variation and Channel Ball involve passing out of contact. These are then developed to bring in a fullback to ensure that there is support for line breaks by the attacking team, and finally, a more tactical game requiring decision making game is used.

FIGURE 10.10 Sample Offloading-in-Contact Rugby-Specific Fitness-Based Practice Plan

	Activity	Coaching points
Warm-up	• Keep Ball (p. 24), three groups of 4v4 at 3 × 1 min. on 20/s off for total of 4 min. • Mobility exercises (e.g., high knees, heel flicks, cariocas, skipping for height), 2 min. • Keep Ball Contact Variation (p. 26), 4 × 45 s on for each team of four • Mobility exercises (e.g., upper body and core), 4 min.	• Encourage accuracy of passing and communication among attackers. • Encourage players to move off the ball and get into space. • Players must stay upright in contact and use footwork to avoid contact.
Main session	• Channel Ball (p. 34), three groups, each group has the ball for 2 min., attacking against the other two groups at two sets per group • Channel Ball variation with fullback (p. 34), three groups, each group has the ball for 2 min., attacking against the other two groups at two sets per group • Spot Game (p. 147), each team has the ball for phases of 3 min. at three times each	• Players must stay upright in contact and look for good passes to players in a better position. • When the line is broken, support players must flood through to give the ball carrier options to pass to. • Players must communicate as a team to work to the spots and create good attacking options at the spots.
Cool-down	• Gentle jog around the pitch stopping at quarter, halfway, corner, and posts to carry out general mobilisation exercises, 5 min. • Static stretches for upper and lower body, 5 min.	• Have players hold each stretch for a minimum of 15 s.

References

Chapter 1 References

Brukner, P., and K. Khan, K. 1994. *Clinical Sports Medicine.* Sydney: McGraw-Hill.

Bunker, D., and R. Thorpe. 1982. "A Model for the Teaching of Games in Secondary Schools." *The Bulletin of Physical Education* 18 (1), 5-8.

Charlesworth, R. 1999. "Designer Games." *Rugby League Coaching Manual* 12: 9-11, 14-17, 19.

Coutts, AJ. 2002. "Use of Skill-Based Games in Fitness Development for Team Sports." *Sports Coach*, 24(4).

Drabik, J. 1996. *Children and Sports Training.* Island Pond, VT: Stadion Publishing Company, pp. 153, 162, 164.

Gabbett, Tim. 2001. "Increasing Training Intensity in Country Rugby League Players." *Rugby League Coaching Magazine* 20, pp. 30-1.

Gabbett, Tim. 2001. "Performance, Fatigue, and Injuries in Rugby League." *Rugby League Coaching Manuals*, p. 22.

Gabbett, Tim J. 2002. "Training Injuries in Rugby League: An Evaluation of Skill-Based Conditioning Games." *Journal of Strength and Conditioning Research* 16 (2), 236-241.

Gabbett, Tim J. 2008. "Do Skill-Based Conditioning Games Offer a Specific Training Stimulus for Junior Elite Volleyball Players?" *Journal of Strength and Conditioning Research* 22 (2), 509-517.

Gabbett, Tim et al. 2006. "Changes in Skill and Physical Fitness Following Training in Talent Identified Volleyball Players." *Journal of Strength and Conditioning Research* 20 (1), 29-35.

Griffen, Linda L., and Joy I. Butler. 2005. *Teaching Games for Understanding.* Champaign, IL: Human Kinetics, pp. 1, 2-4, 52.

Kidman, Lynn. 2001. *Developing Decision Makers: An Empowerment Approach to Coaching.* New Zealand: Innovative Print Communications, Ltd., pp. 25, 35.

Kirk, David, and Ann MacPhail. 2002. "TGfU and Situated Learning." *Journal of Teaching in Physical Education* 21 (2): 177-192.

Launder, Alan. 2003. "Revisit Game Sense." *Sports Coach* 26 (1): 32-34.

Light, Richard. 2004. "Light Up the Sport With Game Sense." *Sports Coach* 26 (2): 33-35.

Martens, Rainer. 2004. *Successful Coaching*, 3rd ed. Champaign, IL: Human Kinetics, p. 172.

Pill, Shane. 2006. "Games Make Sense." *Sports Coach* 29 (3): 10-11.

Slade, Dennis. 2007. "Making First Impressions in Coaching Count Through a TGfU Approach." *Sports Coach* 29 (4): 28-29.

Thorpe, R., and D. Bunker, D. 1989. "A Changing Focus in Games Teaching." In *The Place of Physical Education in Schools,* edited by L. Almond, 42-71. London: Kogan/Page.

Chapter 9 References

Baker, D. 2001. "A Series of Studies on the Training of High Intensity Muscle Power in Rugby League Football Players." *Journal of Strength and Conditioning Research* 15 (2): 198-209.

Baker, D., and S. Nance. 1999. "The Relationship Between Strength and Power in Professional Rugby League Players. *Journal of Strength and Conditioning Research* 13 (3): 224-229.

Baker, D.G., and R.U. Newton. 2004. "An Analysis of the Ratio and Relationship Between Upper Body Pressing and Pulling Strength." *Journal of Strength and Conditioning Research* 18 (3): 594-598.

Baker, Daniel. 2001. "Comparison of Upper Body Strength and Power Between Professional and College-Aged Rugby League Players." *Journal of Strength and Conditioning Research* 15 (1): 30-35.

Balsom, Gaitanos, and Ekblom Soderlund. 1999. "High-Intensity Exercise and Muscle Glycogen Availability in Humans." *Acta Physiologica Scandinavica* 165 (4): 337-345.

doi: 10.1046/j.1365-201x.1999.00517.

Bishop, David. 2001. "Aerobic Interval Training for Team Sport Athletes." *Sports Coach* 23 (4): 27-29.

Brooks, J.H.M., C.W. Fuller, S.P.T. Kemp, and D.B. Reddin. 2005. "A Prospective Study of Injuries and Training Amongst the England 2003 Rugby World Cup Squad." *British Journal of Sports Medicine* 39: 288-293.

Bruce, Lyndell, Damian Farrow, and Warren Young. 2004. Reactive Agility: The Forgotten Aspect of Testing and Training Agility in Team Sport." *Sports Coach* 27 (3): 34-35.

Buttifant D., K. Graham, and K. Cross. 2002. "Agility and Speed in Soccer Players Are Two Different Performance Parameters." In *Proceedings of Science and Football IV,* edited by W. Spinks, T. Reilly, and A. Murphy, 329-332. London & New York: Routledge.

Charlesworth, Ric. 1999. "Designer Games," *Rugby League Coaching Manual* 12: 14-17, 19.

Coutts, Aaron, and Grant Abt. 2005. "Training Aerobic Capacity for Improved Performance in Team Sports. *Sports Coach* 27: 4.

Coutts, A.J., and A.C. Sirotic. 2004. "A Comparison of Small Games Training Versus Interval Training for Improving Aerobic Fitness and Prolonged, High-Intensity, Intermittent Running Performance." Paper presented at the Australian Association of Exercise and Sports Science Inaugural Conference, Brisbane, Australia.

Cunniffe, Brian, Wayne Proctor, Julien S. Baker, and Bruce Davies. 2009. "An Evaluation of the Physiological Demands of Elite Rugby Union Using Global Positioning System Tracking Software." *Journal of Strength and Conditioning Research* 23 (4): 1195-1203.

Djevalikian, R. 1993. "The Relationship Between Asymmetrical Leg Power and Change of Running Direction." Unpublished master's thesis, University of North Carolina, Chapel Hill, NC.

Drust, B., T. Reilly, and N.T. Cable. 2000. "Physiological Responses to Laboratory Based Soccer Specific Intermittent and Continuous Exercise." *Journal of Sports Sciences* 18: 885-892.

Gabbett, Tim. 2001. "Increasing Training Intensity in Country Rugby League Players." *Rugby League Coaching Magazine* 20, p. 16.

Gabbett, Tim. 2005. "Influence of Playing Position on the Site, Nature and Cause of Rugby League Injuries." *Journal of Strength and Conditioning Research* 19 (4): 749-755.

Gabbett, Tim. 2006. "Skill-Based Conditioning Games as an Alternative to Traditional Conditioning for Rugby League Players." *Journal of Strength and Conditioning Research* 20 (2): 309-315.

Gabbett, Tim. 2008. "Influence of Fatigue on Tackling Technique in Rugby League Players." *Journal of Strength and Conditioning Research* 22 (2): 625-632.

Gabbett, Tim. 2009. "Physiological and Anthropometric Correlates of Tackling Ability in R.L. Players." *Journal of Strength and Conditioning Research* 23 (2): 540-548.

Gabbett, Tim, Jason Kelly, and Troy Pezet. 2007. "Rugby League Fitness and Playing Ability." *Journal of Strength and Conditioning Research* 21 (4): 1126-1131.

Gamble, Paul. 2004. "Physical Preparation for Elite Level Rugby Union Football." *Strength and Conditioning Journal* 26 (4): 10-23.

Gleeson, Michael. 2005. *The Powergen Player Energy Report*. Loughborough: Loughborough University.

Helgerud, J. et al. 2001. "Aerobic Endurance Training Improves Soccer Performance." *Medicine and Science in Sport and Exercise* 33 (11): 1925-1931.

Iaua, F. Marcello, Ermanno Rampinini, and Jens Bangsbo. 2009. "High-Intensity Training in Football." *International Journal of Sports Physiology and Performance* l4 (3): 291-306.

International Rugby Board. 2008. *2008 Junior World Championship: Statistical Review and Match Analysis*. Dublin: International Rugby Board.

Kidman, Lynn. 2001. *Developing Decision Makers: An Empowerment Approach to Coaching*. New Zealand: Innovative Print Communications, Ltd., pp. 13-15.

McLean, Ray. 2006. *Any Given Team: Improving Leadership and Team Performance*. Australia: Athlete Development Australia.

Meir, Rudi. 1993. "Evaluating Players' Fitness in Professional Rugby League." *Strength and Conditioning Coach* 1 (4): 11-17.

Meir, R., R. Newton, E. Curtis, M. Fardell, and B. Butler. 2001. "Physical Fitness Qualities of Professional Rugby League Football Players: Determination of Positional Differences." *Journal of Strength and Conditioning Research* 15: 450-458.

Negrete, R., and J. Brophy. 2000. "The Relationship Between Isokinetic Open and Closed Kinetic Chain Lower Extremity Strength and Functional Performance." *Journal of Sports Rehabilitation* 9: 46-61.

O'Connor, D. 1996. "Physiological Characteristics of Professional Rugby League Players." *Strength and Conditioning Coach* 4 (1): 21-26.

Reilly, T., and D. Gilbourne. 2003. "Science and Football: A Review of Applied Research in the Football Codes." *Journal of Sport Sciences* 21 (9): 693-705.

Reilly, T., A.M. Williams, A. Nevill, and A. Franks, A. 2000. "A Multidisciplinary Approach to Talent Identification in Soccer." *Journal of Sports Sciences* 18: 695-702.

Rigg, P., and T. Reilly, T. 1987. "A Fitness Profile and Anthropometric Analysis of First and Second Class Rugby Union Players." In *Proceedings of the First World Congress on Science and Football,* edited by P. Rigg, 194-200. London: E & FN Spon.

Sayers, M. 2000. "Running Techniques for Field Sports Players." *Sports Coach* 23 (1): 26 -27.

Sheppard, J.M., and W.B. Young. 2006. "Agility Literature Review: Classifications, Training and Testing." *Journal of Sports Science* 24: 919-932.

Stone, Keeron J., and Oliver, Jonathan L. 2009. "The Effect of 45 Minutes of Soccer-Specific Exercise on the Performance of Soccer Skills." *International Journal of Sports Physiology and Performance* 4: 163-175.

Thomas, C. 2003. "Review of the Game." In: *IRB* annual report. Dublin: *International Rugby Board*.

Tsitskarsis, G., A. Theoharopoulus, and A. Garefis. 2003. "Speed, Speed Dribble and Agility of Male Basketball Players Playing in Different Positions." *Journal of Human Movement Studies* 45: 21-30.

Walklate, B. et al. 2009. "Supplementing Regular Training with Short-Duration Sprint-Agility Training Leads to a Substantial Increase in Repeated Sprint-Agility Performance with National Level Badminton Players." *Journal of Strength & Conditioning Research* 23 (5): 1477-1481.

Webb, P., and J. Lander. 1983. "An Economical Fitness Testing Battery for High School and College Rugby Teams." *Sports Coach* 7: 44-46.

Young, W., M. Hawken, and L. McDonald. 1996. "Relationship Between Speed, Agility and Strength Qualities in Australian Rules Football." *Strength Conditioning Coach* 4 (4): 3-6.

Young, W.B., R. James, and I. Montgomery. 2002. "Is Muscle Power Related to Running Speed With Changes of Direction?" *Journal of Sports Medicine and Physical Fitness* 42: 282-288.

Young, W.B., M.H. McDowell, and B.J. Scarlett. 2001. "Specificity of Sprint and Agility Training Methods." *Journal of Strength and Conditioning Research* 15: 315-319.

About the Authors

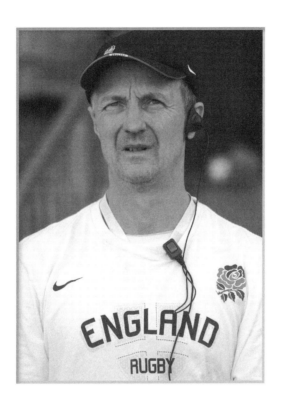

Simon Worsnop is a coach of both rugby union and rugby league and has over 20 years of experience working in the game. Simon is the National Academy fitness adviser for the Rugby Football Union (RFU). In this role, he has worked with England under-19, under-20, and under-21 teams and has been involved with these age groups at six world championships. The holder of several strength and conditioning awards, Simon is both the strength and conditioning coach and an assistant rugby coach in the England under-20 setup. In his coaching role, he seeks to develop games to support team principles and improve individual defensive technique.

Simon has also held a similar role with the Rugby Football League (RFL) and was involved with the full Great Britain, England & England A teams. During his career, Simon has been involved in developing level 1, 2, and 3 certificates in coaching strength and conditioning.

The Rugby Football Union (RFU) is the national governing body for grass-roots and elite rugby in England, with 1,900 autonomous rugby clubs in its membership. The RFU provides over 30,000 coaching sessions each year for its clubs. The clubs have 35 distinct groups, composed of counties, the three armed forces, Oxford and Cambridge universities, the England Schools Rugby Football Union, and England students.